SEMIOTIC
FOUNDATIONS

Advances in Semiotics   *Thomas A. Sebeok, General Editor*

SEMIOTIC FOUNDATIONS

Steps toward an Epistemology of Written Texts

Floyd Merrell

Indiana University Press

BLOOMINGTON

Copyright © 1982 by Floyd Merrell

Manufactured in the United States of America

Library of Congress Cataloging in Publication Data

Merrell, Floyd, 1937–
    Semiotic foundations.

    (Advances in semiotics)
    Includes bibliographical references and index.
    1. Semiotics.   2. Written communication.   I. Title.
II. Series.
P99.M4 1982   001.54'3   81-48631
                                   AACR2

1 2 3 4 5 86 85 84 83 82

ISBN 0-253-35161-8

Contents

PREFACE

A prefatory remark concerning the title of this book is in order. To my knowledge an adequate definition of a "text" does not yet exist. Rather than taking up the arduous task of defining the term, I have, perhaps to the chagrin of the purists who incessantly seek concise definitions before proceeding, chosen simply to set down parameters delineating a specific type of text to be considered. "Written texts," according to the term as it will be used below, entail all corpora written in natural and/or artificial languages for the purpose of conveying observations, ideas, thoughts, intuitions, feelings, and emotions. Verbal discourse in the oral tradition, such as myths and folktales, as well as filmic and other iconic texts, are obviously excluded from this classification. Yet the general class of written texts definitely involves a broad spectrum ranging from poetry through religious, philosophical, and historical works to journalism, and then to reports in the social and physical sciences and even mathematical proofs.[1]

An attempt to establish the "semiotic foundations" of a particular class of physical or mental objects conceived and perceived in texts entails a search for the means and mechanisms by which signs are processed from the most primitive level upward. An inquiry into the "semiotic foundations of written texts" first demands close scrutiny of the act of constructing, at this primitive level, a sign representing something which has no necessary relationship with it—the literal and denotative function of language—or representing something, which it might ordinarily not represent—the figurative and connotative function of language. Second, the grapheme, or the written mark, must be carefully considered insofar as it is the visual counterpart of an auditory sign the meaning of which is presumably synonymous with that of the written sign. Yet, since the visual sign remains as a temporal artifact after it is constructed and perceived, it can be re-perceived or reiterated as if irrespective of time and memory. With each reiteration, however, and as shall be illustrated below, there is a manifested *difference,* which is nevertheless ordinarily conceived as sameness, or even identity. Yet precise sameness or identity does not and cannot prevail in what will be described as a world of increasing *differentiation.* Hence the task is ultimately to determine how conception and perception of the written sign, in spite of our Western world view, resist categorization according to traditional Aristotelian principles.

I do not begin this study of written texts with a critical survey of the Russian formalist-structuralists, the French structuralists and post-structuralists, the so-called "text grammarians," or Anglo-American theorists of literary texts. Books abound that summarize previous theories of, and methods for analyzing, texts, especially artistic texts. One more such book would contribute little. My objective is to inquire, from a broad epistemological view, into the underlying nature of the conception and perception of all written texts. Since I begin at the most rudimentary level of consciousness, where the sign is marked off and distinguished from all other potential and actual signs in the world, the first stages of this inquiry will treat signs in general, rather than more specifically the written sign. In addition, at this primordial level of consciousness, as I will illustrate and as Peirce constantly reminds us, any dividing line between animal and human semiotic activity becomes well-nigh indistinguishable.[2] Consequently, I find that I cannot avoid using examples from zoosemiotics on building, from the ground level upward, a hierarchy of increasingly sophisticated systems of signs culminating in written texts.[3] It might for this reason appear that the level of exposition in the first chapters of this book has little or no direct relevance to the more traditional notion of written texts. Nonetheless, I feel it is necessary to establish the essential groundwork for the pages that follow.

Furthermore, if the perspective maintained in this inquiry is to be epistemological in the broadest sense, then a preliminary word also be said to justify the inclusion of poetical, philosophical, religious, and other "subjective" texts along with scientific texts. Early in this century the logical positivists set out to eliminate all metaphysical claims of knowledge. Even Popper, who departed from the positivist camp, still maintained in *The Logic of Scientific Discovery* (1959, 15) that: "The central problem of epistemology has always been and still is the problem of the growth of knowledge. *And the growth of knowledge can be studied best by studying the growth of scientific knowledge.*" Since the 1950s, however, logical positivism has come under sustained attack by scholars from diverse backgrounds.[4] In general a new approach to the philosophy of science has followed, which entails "a rejection of formal logic as the primary tool for the analysis of science, and its replacement by a reliance on detailed study of the history of science" (H.I. Brown, 1977, 9–10). Moreover, science has begun to yield its privileged position as the repository of all human knowledge, and in accord with earlier philosophers from diverse backgrounds such as Cassirer and Whitehead, it is being recognized that other forms of cognition, including myth, religion, and the arts, embody a form of knowledge which, although not necessarily competing with scientific knowledge, is equally valid. Nevertheless, I still find it necessary to introduce a large number of ideas and concepts from contemporary physics and the philosophy of science to illustrate my conjectures. I do not wish to impress on the reader that the scientists and philosophers of science have all the answers for the semioticians. Simply, epistemology enjoys the longest tradition in these disciplines. Hence I believe they can corroborate many concepts useful to the theoretician of semiotics.

It is undoubtedly apparent that I place semiotic theory at the border of broad philosophical issues. This is necessary and ultimately inevitable. A survey of radical breakthroughs in various disciplines—Einstein and Planck in physics, Piaget in psychology, Lévi-Strauss in anthropology, Chomsky in linguistics—leads one to the conclusion that the recent trend in theory-making has been away from narrow positivist and behaviorist views of cognition and toward theories grounded in general metaphysical issues. Even generic theories of semiotics proposed to date—for example, Bateson's from one perspective, Derrida's from another, and to a lesser degree Eco's—draw from long-standing philosophical problems.[5] Certainly Sebeok's "mopping-up work" in his *Contributions to the Doctrine of Signs* (1976b) and elsewhere is necessary, useful, and, as he rightly points out, can "prove quite fascinating in the execution." Yet I believe that after such preparatory work, the time has come to scrutinize the disciplines whose interests are at least in part compatible with those of the semiotician, and, by drawing key ideas from these disciplines, to begin construction of a viable epistemological, and ultimately a theoretical, framework. Consequently, what I attempt to develop here is a broad epistemologically based theoretical introduction to future semiotic considerations of written texts. This book is designed not only for the specialist, but also for the student of philosophy, literature, or linguistics generally interested in the conception and perception of written texts.

Given my interdisciplinary perspective, I have necessarily drawn from a variety of sources to the extent that this book might appear to be a smorgasbord of ideas. But there is an overriding direction that ultimately gives it coherence. And this overriding direction is pointed out by an elaborate set of "thought experiments" designed to illustrate—i.e., to show in the Wittgensteinian sense—my assumptions and conjectures. As such, they are not "thought experiments" in the strict scientific sense. In their composite form they are akin to scientific models, but at the same time they possess explanatory power at an intuitive or experiential level. According to Peirce's definition of signs, they are primarily *icons* insofar as there is a spatial, even topological, similarity between the image (signifier) ideally created by the "thought experiment" and the denotatum (the concept being illustrated). Simultaneously, they are in part *indexes*, since the image is necessarily contiguous (i.e., juxtaposed) with the concept. In this manner, the "thought experiments'" iconic function provides for their modeling ability; their indexical function potentially allows for an intuitive grasp of the set of relations between image and concept, and between "thought experiment" and "thought experiment."

The reader might be surprised by the method used in presenting these "thought experiments": a list of injunctions demanding that he re-create for himself the original experience, which led to the book's writing. Such an unorthodox method—that is, unorthodox at least in the humanities—is not without value. By following the implicit or explicit injunctions in a musical score, a cake recipe, a mathematical proof, or even when "getting inside" a poem, re-experiencing by doing is the surest route toward understanding, although indirectly, an original experience. In such cases, the experience, rather than an explicitly formulated description, incorporates the meaning. Hence these "thought experiments" are themselves signs that on referring to and illustrating other signs, become part of Peirce's notion of the indefinite and ongoing flux of semiosis.

Finally, I have, for emphasis, punctuated this book with four "axioms," six "propositions," and seven "corollaries." By no means do I pretend to have attained any level of mathematical rigor. I merely use these aphoristic statements as pivotal points for constructing the "thought experiments" and developing subsequent arguments. This unavoidably makes for a sometimes pithy style that instead of being direct and to the point, becomes tangential, in accord with the above-mentioned *iconic-indexical* functions. Consequently, on reading this book perhaps it is advisable for the reader to bear in mind the set of relations between the "axioms," "propositions," and "corollaries," rather than trying to assimilate the argument in the traditional cumulative fashion. When read in such a way the experience derived should be, given obvious differences, similar to that of obeying the implicit injunctions when listening to a piece of music, when submerging oneself in a poem, or when following the explicit injunctions in a mathematical proof. The real "proof," whether musical, poetic, or mathematical, lies in human experience, not in the physics of sound, the theory of metrics, or rules for combining numbers.

Introduction

0.10 A preliminary sketch of three premises is essential before beginning this inquiry.

0.11 The power to abstract is not the sole dominion of the Western world mind, or even of man. All organisms abstract whether aware of the fact or not. "Innate response mechanisms" enable lower animals to recognize not particular features but classes of combinations that induce preparedness for one, two, or more possible responses that are definable also as abstractions (Thorpe, 1963). In the human organism such concepts as "unconscious inference" (von Helmholtz, 1971), "abductions" (Peirce, 1960), "inferential constructs" (Bartlett, 1958), "tacit inference" (Polanyi, 1964), and "hypothetico-deductive reasoning" (Popper, 1959) testify that the mind possesses some form of abstractive organizing capacity. By means of this organizing capacity the mind methodically selects (abstracts) from the real world of objects, acts, and events that which can be correlated with human biological needs, culture-bound world views and conceptual frameworks, and personal idiosyncrasies (Hayek, 1969).

With respect to the human organism, this power of abstraction can progress from conscious to nonconscious activity. For example, an expert chess player can rapidly and without much effort memorize the configuration of pieces on a chess board as long as it represents a possible state of affairs in the game and is organized according to explicitly defined rules; that is, insofar as the configuration falls within his expectations of what constitutes the range of possible configurations. In contrast, if he is shown a "random" arrangement, he will only with great difficulty be able to commit it to memory (Groot, 1966). His knowledge of what constitutes a "logical" arrangement of chess pieces, like his knowledge of walking, riding a bicycle, driving a car, playing a piano, etc., has become enbedded in his consciousness. Such embedded knowledge enables one to exercise highly complicated skills apparently "without even thinking," since one need not possess immediate awareness of each aspect of the skill (for other similar examples and further discussion, see Koestler, 1964; Polanyi, 1958; Merrell, 1980b, 1980c; Ryle, 1949).

Apparently, part of our power to abstract precedes perception: It is inborn (Popper, 1972). With respect to human cognition, this line of reasoning follows recent anti-inductivist theories of knowledge that claim that the capacity of the mind to generalize (abstract) comes first, and that one does not simply generalize from a conglomeration of particular experiences in Baconian fashion. In other words, the sensory world does not simply feed information from which the mind selects and derives abstractions; the mind possesses a priori remarkable capabilities for abstraction that enable it to experience particulars from within a whole structural framework it has abstracted from its world. In this sense, one's experienced world, like a scientific theory, necessarily omits much detail. And, like a scientific theory, this experienced world is automatically and tacitly filtered through a classificatory grid.

A human being devoid of such selective processes might be a perfect "nominalist" who, like Luria's aphasic (1968) or Borges' "Funes the Memorious" (1964), could with his photographic memory retain all of what he perceived, even to the most minute detail. But he would be incapable of generalizing, like a machine that assimilates tremendous quantities of information in a linear stream without the capacity to relate that information to other items of information it has stored in its memory bank.

Hence, premise one: KNOWING HOW TO ABSTRACT IS A FORM OF INBORN KNOWLEDGE OF WHICH AN ORGANISM,

HUMAN OR ANIMAL, CAN BE ONLY AT MOST PARTIALLY AWARE.

0.12 Non-inborn human knowledge, acquired from within a cultural context, is explicitly conveyed primarily through speech and writing. The question that is considered in the following chapters is: What is the relationship between the knowing process and the conception and perception of written texts?

One approach to the problem of knowledge entails what is called the "logical justification" of knowledge. It involves reducing a body of knowledge into some sort of "logical" order such that, from a fundamental set of atomic propositions, more and more complex levels can be derived—a method commensurate with the "logical atomism" of Russell (1956), the early Wittgenstein (1961), and the logical positivists. The problem with this approach is that it considers knowledge to be an established fact—what is presently known and recorded for posterity—rather than an ongoing process of knowing and of rejecting or correcting what is known. In other words, according to this royal road to knowledge, truth is simply what corresponds to the facts (see Popper, 1959, following Tarski, 1956). The problem is that it is an ethnocentric view, for the facts are invariably to an extent interpreted a priori (Crick, 1976).[1] This tacit interpretation occurs not only at the biological level, but to an extent it is also dependent upon certain language-bound, culture-bound, and even private idiosyncratic imperatives.[2]

According to a contemporary and more adequate approach to the problem, knowing is a process believed ultimately to rest at some precognitive, and hence nonconscious, level of experience.[3] By means of some precognitive mechanism, each human being internalizes, in interaction with his environment, a hypothesis concerning what the world is—must be—like, and he constantly attempts to correlate his highly selective empirical world with it. This internalized hypothesis allows him to make discriminations in his field of experience, the forms of which are ultimately grounded in the precognitive mechanism. And his knowledge is derived from the particular set of discriminations that are made. Yet at the same time the content of these discriminations is determined chiefly by his particular environment-bound social and psychological needs. Consequently, his internalized hypothesis, and therefore his knowledge, is continually being altered, reorganized, and corrected. In this sense, his knowledge does not rest on a fundamental set of absolute and invariant truths. It is, more properly speaking, relative to his culture, his world view, and his language.[4]

The second premise is, in this light: THE KNOWING PROCESS INVOLVES ONGOING AND DYNAMIC INTERACTION BE-TWEEN THE INDIVIDUAL, HIS SOCIETY, AND HIS PER-CEIVED WORLD.

0.13 What do we do when we write? Put marks on paper that represent speech, as Saussure (1966) tells us? If this is the case it is by extension true that writing is subordinated to spoken language. A universal opposition is usually assumed to exist between *langue* and *parole,* the latter consisting in the oral mode, which can serve as a model for the written mode. But does it logically follow that the semiotic of writing is merely a graphemic reproduction of the semiotic of speaking? What about the possibility of a triad: *langue/parole/ecriture?*[5]

Speech is a flow. There are no necessary "bits" of speech acts, although speech has, at the phonemic level, been analyzed into "bits" of information, albeit with some controversy (Jakobson and Halle, 1956; Jakobson, Fant, and Halle, 1964). In contrast, "bits" are overtly manifested in linear, Western world writing. In fact, I conjecture below that it is possible to break speech acts into "bits" and analyze them effectively only by virtue of the prior existence of a phonetic-based system of writing. Analysis, according to this notion, depends chiefly, though not exclusively, on a special characteristic possessed by writing—a characteristic most common, once again, to Western world communities.

In an oral culture the flow of speech is unidimensional, linear, and temporal; speech possesses no true spatial dimensions unless it is given graphic representation. Individuals in this oral culture combine "bits" of information into larger meaningful wholes when they speak because they have, chiefly nonconsciously, internalized the rules for such combinations. They know how to do it ordinarily without being able to tell us explicitly how it is that they know how. That is to say, the types and categories built up by the "bits" of speech they use always existed but not necessarily at conscious levels.

On the other hand, when a linguist discovers the types and categories used in speech, and the ordering of sentences into subject, verb, object, and so on, he must be explicitly aware of necessary boundaries, of domains, and of distinctions and oppositions between domains. Formal logic, mathematics, formulation of propositions and rules of argumentation, are likewise closely tied to such a form of explicit awareness. Moreover, if certain mathematicians, logicians, and philosophers are correct in telling us that they are engaged in making explicit that which was always implicit, then their activity is in essence similar to that of the linguist who must be aware of grammar rules and language use, of types and categories. This might help to account for the fact that, though oral cultures have developed remarkably complex and sophisticated systems of classification (Lévi-Strauss, 1966) and elaborately interwoven structures in their myths (Lévi-Strauss, 1969) and language (Whorf, 1956), they appear little inclined toward the Western disciplines of mathematics, abstract science, and logic, or even linguistics. The capacity is, of course, there, and certain of the knowledge is present, but at implicit levels.[6]

Explicitly formulated grounds for knowledge in the Western world sense (i.e., the generation of proofs and propositions, and logical rules of argumentation) depend upon relatively context-free modes of communication. And this knowledge is, in the Western tradition, most adequately conveyed through graphic symbols— that is, linear phonetic-based symbols. By means of graphic representation in written texts, tables and lists can be constructed, boundaries can be more easily sharpened, taxonomies can be more effectively built, hierarchies can be established, and sets of symbols can be readily separated out and juxtaposed, compared, and contrasted; in short, they can be analyzed. In addition, by means of these abstractive activities, explicit rules can eventually be formulated that specify this two-dimensional visual and graphic order of things. The linear and unidimensional nature of spoken "texts," in contrast, requires that they be internalized and used in relatively more tacit and implicit ways. Consequently, analysis in oral traditions must rely chiefly on memory, which is extremely fallible, and therefore explicit knowledge through conscious analysis of messages is relatively limited.

The essence of premise three, which will be discussed in more detail below, is: SPEECH AND WRITING PERTAIN TO COMPLEMENTARY MODES, ALTHOUGH THERE EXIST INTERDEPENDENCY AND INTERACTION BETWEEN THEM.[7]

Chapter 1
Steps toward a Foundation
of Boundaried Spaces

1.10 Preliminaries

1.11 Begin in the beginning with the unboundaried. (The unboundaried is not the same as infinite and empty space [nothingness] or infinitely divisible time. Space and time are "states of consciousness," "constructions of the mind." They do not exist as such until they have become boundaried entities.) First, consider the act of boundarying space.

1.12 Mark off (in the mind) an enclosed space, something like this: $\bigcirc$.[1] Boundaried space has now come into existence by virtue of the boundary that marred the unboundaried. The mark distinguishes the space within from the space without. Call the distinguishing characteristic between the space within and the space without a *difference*.[2]

Cross over into the marked-off boundary and you are now inside. Recross it and you are outside. Crossing and then recrossing is the same as if you had not crossed at all. This can be written as: $\emptyset$ = _____(where "/" denotes the nullification of the crossing and "_____" denotes the unboundaried).

Now, mark off the boundaried space, and then mark off another one. The two spaces together have the same potential value as if only one space had been marked off. This can be written as: $\bigcirc \, \bigcirc$ = $\bigcirc$.[3] Hence:

AXIOM I. *To mark off a boundaried space and then to mark off the same boundaried space again is the same as to mark off the boundaried space.*

Axiom II. *To cross the boundary and then to recross it is the same as not crossing it* (see Spencer-Brown, 1969).[4]

1.20 "Thought Experiments"

1.21 The following "experiments" progress from relatively primitive "boundaried spaces," where presumably no or little "consciousness" is involved, to increasingly complex boundaried spaces that include animal forms of "consciousness." Propositions concerning construction of boundaried spaces by the human mind must await later developments.

1.22 Put some iron filings on a heavy piece of paper and place a magnet below the paper. Tap the paper slightly with a pencil, causing it to vibrate. Most of the filings will be arranged in a definite pattern. A primitive form of "boundaried space" has been marked off in nature. It has definite form; it is a formation, but it represents no information. The role of the iron filings was completely passive. They sought no information, and, after their formation into the pattern, their future behavior was not altered.

The filings established a state of equilibrium, the most probable and the most tensionless state of existence. But this equilibrium was that of a closed, static system. Take away the magnet and the pattern remains the same. The filings are incapable of regrouping themselves into their original state. They are incapable of self-organization. There is no discernible purpose, no goal, no plan. *Entropy* prevails.

For the existence of information there must be a receiver that seeks information or whose behavior is changed, although ever so slightly, after the information is received. This, as will be seen, implies an open, dynamic system wherein *negentropy* increases (Schrödinger, 1945). This first "experiment" represents the lowest possible index of organization (or disorganization). There is one and only one possible response to a particular change in the environment (that is, when the filings are observed with respect to their macroscopic properties).

1.23 Place a potted plant in a room near a window facing south (that is, if you are in the Northern Hemisphere). The sunlight penetrating the room becomes for the plant the representation of a sort of primitive "boundaried space." It is the necessary information for the construction of that "boundaried space." The plant invariably turns its future growth toward the window. Although this growth represents a negentropic state, there seems to be for the plant little or no alternative, no choice. Plant "behavior," unlike animal behavior, is severely limited in three ways: (a) plants, with few exceptions, possess no forms of locomotion, (b) plants have no nervous system, and (c) plants exercise relatively little action upon their environment (Piaget, 1978). The next step up the hierarchy is the level of the lower animal forms.

1.24 Imagine a hungry flatworm. If it senses food a boundaried space is established, or crossed. The organism queried its environment and part of that environment sent back the desired information. The flatworm eats. Now consider the same organism that is no longer hungry. It senses food and "simultaneously" crosses and re-crosses the established boundary without acting on its environment. The prevailing state of affairs is as if the boundary had never existed in the first place. There is little or no temporality involved, only boundaried space. The organism's response to the boundaried spaces it crosses depends upon its inner needs or desires that are largely to totally biological. The organism can choose either to eat or not to eat. This is an all-or-nothing "digital" choice as in the previous case. But the parameters of choice are broader than a simple yes/no affair. It can eat more or less according to its needs. This latter choice rests at the "analog" level.[5]

1.25 Think of an opossum being pursued by a carnivorous animal. Let the image of the fleeing animal represent a boundaried space for the pursuer. This space denotes something like "Alive and kicking" or "Food." Suddenly the opossum goes limp "as if" it were dead. Let this state be represented by an equal and opposite boundaried space that denotes the equivalent of "Dead," which can be represented by: $-\bigcirc$. Combining the spaces produces no space: $\bigcirc + \left(-\bigcirc\right) =$ _____. (Notice that this is the same as crossing and then recrossing a boundaried space.) Consequently the pursuer gives up its chase after some "questioning" of the situation.

In this case a signal, or a boundaried space, is manifested, which denotes the opposite of what the original signal denotes; hence the original signal is in a sense "negated." The pursuing animal has one of two alternatives: continue the attack or stop the attack. In addition to the continuous, "analog" nature of the signals, the system is necessarily "digital": It does or it does not elicit a particular response.

1.26 Now consider a case unlike the previous one, which involves members of the same species: a family of herring gulls (Count, 1969).

When a nestling pecks at a red spot on the parent's bill it expects food. Let this signal-sign be a boundaried space. This space denotes something like, "Please feed me." The female also solicits sexual attention from the male by the same signal-sign. Let this signal-sign be the same boundaried space, which denotes the equivalent of, "I want sex." This boundaried space is, so to speak, "ambiguous." The female may intend to say, "I want sex," but the male interprets the message as, "Please feed me." The female consequently can accept the food or not, but it cannot talk about the meaning of the message. It cannot say, "No, you idiot. What I wanted was sex." This is necessarily the case since the iconic boundaried space allows no true negation unless it is juxtaposed with an opposite space such as in 1.25.

1.27 Observe a hive of bees. When a worker bee returns it immediately opens its scent gland, which serves as an "analog" signal, a boundaried space, to the guard bees denoting membership to the hive. A foreign worker displays a distinct odor that causes bellicose behavior from the guards. Each boundaried space elicits a choice of "digital" responses: attack or not attack. But one boundaried space denotes the opposite of what the other denotes. That is, one is a countersignal or counterspace of the other. A countersignal solicits a response other than what would ordinarily be solicited. Similar countersignals consist in the "marks" that wolves place over previous "marks" at given "odor posts" along a trail (Sebeok, 1972). Such "marks" signal to another wolf that a visit has been paid by friend or foe, a female in search of a mate, or a young, old, healthy, or sick animal. These countersignals serve as a rudimentary form of "metacommunication" about a set of "digital" responses (Sebeok, 1972). That is, they represent signals that are sent out at the level of the coding device itself about the relations between addresser and addressee. Other more common forms of metacommunicative devices involve play activity, as will be observed in a later section.

1.28 For a lower animal the smell of food is an "analog" *signal* for the presence of food. At a more sophisticated level, a closed peanut shell is like an *index* that indicates that a peanut is inside. Nut-eating animals instinctively know what it indicates and how to get at the morsel of food that lies within. A chimp, in addition, can easily be taught that a peanut is inside a small box marked with, say, an *x* (Pribram, 1971). This is an arbitrarily chosen "nonbiological" symbol that represents a relatively high degree of abstraction. However, confusion, at this primitive level of sign activity, can and often does occur when a "digital" leap is enacted at this and other levels of abstraction.

Take for example Pavlov's dog. It habitually reacts to the olfactory *signal* for food by salivating. Later it learns to associate a bell with food, and thereafter the bell, an arbitrarily chosen *index,* elicits the salivatory response even though the food is not present. The arbitrary and abstract *index* is confused with a biological *signal.* This "mental shortcut" is convenient as long as the arbitrary *index* remains as part of the dog's conventional world. If not the animal may be placed in a quandary since its expectations concerning that *index* are not satisfied. It might even become "neurotic" (Leach, 1976). A similar case is that of the dog that can be taught to differentiate between a circular sign and an oval sign. If the two shapes are changed in such a way that they become more and more alike the dog shows "neurotic" tendencies when confronted with this ambiguous situation (Bateson, 1972).

1.29 Now, the activities I have been describing above can be placed in a hierarchy:

(a) 1–1 RELATIONS. There may be one and only one response to a given situation, with no information sought and no subsequent negentropic increase in the system (the iron filings), or information can be passively received without being sought, and a subsequent response to that information brings about negentropic increase but entails little or no choice (the plant).

(b) 1-2a RELATIONS. Information is sought, and a simple positive or negative choice may be exercised at the discretion of the biological needs of the organism with a subsequent change in the environment as a result of the organism's action on it (the flatworm).

(c) 1-2b RELATIONS. A ("metaphorical") message may be sent out by the addressing organism from which there can be response of a simple positive or negative nature by the addressee. This message leads to a greater or lesser degree of change in behavior on the part of addresser and addressee (the opossum, the bee, etc.).

(d) 1-2c RELATIONS. A message may be conveyed that induces one of a complementary pair of possible responses that are not simply positive or negative but represent mutually contradictory alternatives (the gull, etc.).

(e) 2-1 RELATIONS. Two different messages of different levels of abstraction are conveyed that can induce the same response ("peanuts in a shell," Pavlov's dog, etc.).

1.30 Preliminaries (Continued)

1.31 Re-create a boundaried space and simultaneously give it a *name*.[6] The name particularizes the space within. It gives it a value. To name is to sort, divide, *differentiate*, order; it is to validate the *differentiating* boundary in which a space is constructed. "Knowledge" derives from the activity of naming and from the possession of names. A boundary cannot be marked off without creating a *difference,* and knowledge is not acquired without marking off boundaries. A boundary is in the beginning no more than a simple (analog) *icon:* It has no tense, no syntax, no negation, no modal markers. It is simply there to *differentiate* positively and all at once, or if not there it *differentiates* not at all.

1.32 Assume that the name of the space is *x*, like the peanut in the box. *x* is not the space nor is it the same as the space. Hence *x* remains necessarily outside the circumference of the boundaried space: $\bigcirc$ + *x*.

1.33 But *x* is not always separable from the space. *x* and the space combine to form an entity that may be called a *sign.* That is, in the formation of the sign, *x* (an expression or image), combines with the space (a content or concept) to form what is ordinarily conceived to be an indissoluble whole. Therefore: $\bigcirc$ + *x* → $\bigcirc$◡*x* (where "→" denotes "becomes" or "is transformed into," and "◡" denotes the ordinarily inseparable bond between space and name).[7]

1.34 Say "*x*." On so evoking a name or a word, you automatically cross the boundary *differentiating* that which is inside from that which is outside. You are inside the space. Say "*x*" once again. You are already inside, so repeating the name is the same as saying the name only once.[8] Therefore: $\bigcirc$◡*x* + $\bigcirc$◡*x* = $\bigcirc$◡*x*. Also, since to say the word implies crossing the boundary, you can cross the boundary without saying the word but you cannot say the word without crossing the boundary.

1.35 To cross the boundary of the space at a given point and then to recross it without evoking simultaneously the name of the space is the same as not crossing it at all. Unboundaried space is boundaried by marking off a given domain. This boundary is qualified by giving it a name. The name creates a boundary that can be relatively permanent or ephemeral depending upon whether the boundary is recrossed or not. The name is not the thing (the space) but it is in a certain way interchangeable with the thing named. This is because the thing named is a *difference* in the otherwise undifferentiated and unboundaried, and the name is a *difference* existing outside the differentiated space in what remains undifferentiated and unboundaried. For example, to replace x by a circle is to combine the space named with a second space that was previously the name existing in the unboundaried. This combination is the same as the space. That is:

$$\bigcirc \smile x \rightarrow \bigcirc\bigcirc = \bigcirc.$$

However, the name is not directly reducible to the space; only when replaced by a space lying contiguously with another "equal" space is the above reduction to one space possible. Notice that it is the spaces that have been condensed or reduced. The name has not been fused into a space to "disappear" into a space, nor is the name merely equal to or the same as the space. To confuse the name with the thing named (the space) is like, in a materialistic sense, confusing the map with the territory, the word with the thing, or Pavlov's dog confusing the signal and the index.

Since names are in this formal sense replaceable by spaces lying contiguously with respect to the spaces represented by those names, it can be said that the *sign* is in the beginning arbitrary. That is, the name represents a space and can be replaced by a space, but at the same time it is necessarily something indeterminately other than the space. And the combination of the name and the space (the sign) can represent an object, act, or event in the world, but at the same time the sign is something indeterminately other than that object, act, or event.[9]

1.36 Now, say "not x." On so doing you have introduced negation. That is, combining the evocation "x" with "not x" results in the unboundaried. Hence: $x + \text{not } x = $ _____.[10]

Recrossing the pure space can produce the unboundaried. In contrast, "not x" gives the same result by means of something other than either the space or the opposite of the space. Such negation would be impossible for the organism capable only of constructing boundaried spaces.[11] Hence:

AXIOM III. *To name and then to name again is the same as to name.*

AXIOM IV. *To name a boundaried space and then to negate the name of that boundaried space is the same as to not name the boundaried space* (see Spencer-Brown, 1972).

COROLLARY I: *To mark off successive boundaries is to move in the direction of increasing organizational complexity* (see Laszlo, 1972).

1.37 What is meant by the "increasing organizational complexity" in Corollary I? Precisely this: The sign's initial arbitrariness allows for a potentially unlimited number of variations by the organism capable of altering boundaried spaces and names of boundaried spaces at will. I will attempt to demonstrate during the course of this inquiry that the human organism alone possesses this capacity for such a potentially unlimited generation of variations.[12]

Chapter 2
The Invention of Our Mental Worlds

2.10 Perception Is Perspectival

2.11 Let us now transport our focus of interest to the uniquely human realm of perception. Then in Chapter 3, we will return to a primitive level of sign foundations in order to understand this distinctly human semiotic.

2.12 Imagine that I draw this representation of a boundaried space:

Figure 1

"It is a man," you say. Since faces of men exist in our world we can conclude that the drawing denotes something: *a* man. Then I declare, "That is a drawing of Richard Nixon." If you agree, it can now be said that the picture denotes something more specific: *that* man, whose existence in the physical world is real. Now, of course, slightly and mediately before you named the set of marks-on-paper I drew, you constructed an inner boundaried space of which it is the material representation. The name you attached to the boundaried space gives it a value, and as such it can be presumed to correspond to something in the physical world. But the problem is this: The boundaried space is never exactly identical with its material manifestation, the marks-on-paper, and it is certainly not the same as the real thing.

The marks-on-paper, a caricature, are necessarily a very rough selective abstraction, and the boundaried space is, let us say, a conceptual abstraction. But the real thing in the physical world is concrete. In its myriad complexity, it is *in toto* indescribable, for the natural physical world contains no abstractions. Consequently, your "inner" space can have no faithful and direct counterpart "outside."

2.13 However, what if there were no men in the physical world? Or better, what if, for instance, I had drawn a caricature of a unicorn? In this case would we remark that it is a drawing that denotes nothing? Or that the drawing's denotation is null? Or that it represents nothing? Yet how can we agree that the picture is of a unicorn and at the same time that it represents nothing? Certainly we will concede that the marks-on-paper are of something, that this something is a unicorn, and that it cannot be at the same time nothing. If we admit that this something is a unicorn we have simultaneously admitted that it is something of some sort or other. Even to declare that it is nothing is to admit, by using the copula, that it possesses some kind of reality.

What kind of reality might this be? Well, if a boundaried space can be constructed for a unicorn, if a name can be attached to it, and if a picture-as-marks-on-paper can represent it, but if no physical world representation exists for it, then the only reality it can enjoy is "mental."[1] That is, the boundaried space, a "mental reality," can correspond to the name and the marks-on-paper, but not to any existent thing in the physical world.

However, this "mental reality" of boundaried spaces within which the unicorn can be embodied is not absolutely divorced from what we ordinarily believe to be our "real world," for "horses" and "horns" exist, yet they do not exist in such a combination.[2] In order to illustrate this assertion, let us consider a painting of a landscape. It must, of course, always be something other than the actual landscape as well as something other than its name or the set of names labeling its parts. But what is more important, it will never be equal, in its totality, to the artist's original set of conceptualized boundaried spaces he constructed when, with a flash of insight, he conceived the work. Try as he may, the actual brush-strokes-on-canvas will never be exactly what he had in mind. Something, as he well knows but cannot remedy to his complete satisfaction, is always missing. Certainly, the set of boundaried spaces is at least incompletely portrayed in the work of art, all or parts of which can be named, and which ordinarily correspond to some aspect of the physical world. But, to repeat, the spaces can be no more than an abstract representation of a given part of the physical world, or of the painting.

The point to be made is this: If the boundaried spaces of a unicorn can be in the mind, but a unicorn presumably cannot exist in the physical world, and if the artist's initial set of boundaried spaces can be, momentarily at least, in his mind, but only incompletely portrayed as brush-strokes-on-canvas, then the boundaried space of a unicorn and the artist's flash of insight (an intrinsically constructed set of boundaried spaces) enjoy a comparable form of "reality." Both consist in a set of particulars that correspond to parts or all of existent things in the physical world. But in their totality, neither can have direct referents in that world. And this "reality," which the boundaried space of a unicorn and the artist's initial insight share, is appropriately "mental."

2.14 Let us extrapolate briefly from the above examples to a new level of generalization in order to illustrate the abstract characteristic of boundaried spaces. Then we will renew our discussion of the more fundamental level of perception before returning to an even deeper level in Chapter 3: the foundations of signs.

The "mental reality" of a work of art is comparable to certain types of scientific theories. Some scientific theories can be built upon visualizable models (i.e., the planetary model of the atom). In contrast, it is not possible intuitively to represent other theories by pictures or visual images (i.e., the quantum mechanical model). The first case is similar to the above "face" example or to the artist's incomplete portrayal—models-by-analogy (see Hesse, 1966). The second case is more interesting, however, and it illustrates how boundaried spaces constructed during scientific activity can reach a new level of abstraction (see Duhem, 1962; Popper, 1972). For instance, quantum mechanics, as well as relativity theory, avail themselves of $\sqrt{-1}$ for their formulations. But $\sqrt{-1}$ is nonvisualizable; that is, there are no correlates for it in the physical world, and therefore there can be no adequate "mental" pictures constructed to represent either quantum mechanics or relativity theory (Schrödinger, 1958; Heisenberg, 1958). Of course, boundaried spaces for $\sqrt{-1}$ can be represented by marks (mathematical notations), but, unlike the unicorn or the artist's insight, they cannot be represented by pictures-as-marks-on-paper that at least partly correspond to real things in the physical world. Through mathematical notations, moreover, the physicist can indirectly account for an exceedingly abstracted portion of reality, but he cannot adequately talk about it in his natural language. Yet he eventually must resort to his natural language, especially when explaining his findings to the layman. On so attempting to speak, the best he can do, however, is use words that produce vague and ambiguous pictures in the mind that can have no more than equally vague and ambiguous connections with reality (Heisenberg, 1958).[3] Thus his description will always and inexorably remain incomplete.

Interestingly enough, the physicist's problem, due to the increased level of abstraction, is somewhat the inverse of that of the artist. The latter, during his creative flash of insight, conceived/perceived a set of boundaried spaces with pristine clarity, but, after the fact, he could give those boundaried spaces no more than incomplete representation. The former, possessing a concise descriptive language, can rather effectively account for a very limited domain constituting part of physical reality, but the boundaried spaces constructed with this language cannot be represented in more than an incomplete, ambiguous, and vague way by means of boundaried spaces constructed with a natural language that enjoys correlates in the physical world. Yet, let us suppose that the physicist himself also experienced an initial flash of insight upon conceiving his abstract formulation; i.e., when he intuited the union between a set of mathematical boundaried spaces and some aspect of the physical world. These mathematical spaces are somehow "real," just as the artist's insight was "real," yet in both cases the relationship between them and the physical world remains unfaithful, partly ineffable, and over the long haul, incomprehensible.

With respect to the use of mathematics in science, Wigner (1969, 139) tells us:

> The miracle of the appropriateness of the language of mathematics for the formulation of the laws of physics is a wonderful gift which we neither understand nor deserve. We would be grateful for it and hope that it will remain valid in future research and that it will extend, for better or for worse, to our pleasure even though perhaps also to our bafflement, to wide branches of learning.

If we juxtapose this quotation with a paraphrase of it that is directed to the arts, we obtain striking results:

The miracle of the appropriateness of novel and creative constructs in the arts for the formulation of aesthetically pleasing works is a wonderful gift which we neither understand nor deserve. We should be grateful for it and hope that it will remain valid in future artistic endeavors and that it will extend, for better or for worse, to our pleasure even though perhaps also to our bafflement, to wide branches of learning.

Artistic creativity through relatively concrete images, as well as scientific creativity by means of mathematical language, entail the discovery of unity in what was disorderly. The outer world is chaos—infinite variety. Yet instants of creative insight occur when this chaos is ordered. Consequently, during such instants boundaried spaces are, whether in the sciences or the arts, combined to reveal hidden likenesses and correspondences that were not previously known.

2.15 Finally, we begin to perceive the necessary abstractness of all boundaried spaces at the deepest level: the physicist's mathematical spaces and the pure, uncluttered spaces of the artist's insight, all of which share, it appears, a common "reality."[4] Boundaried spaces, then, are *forms*, enjoying no necessary *content*. That is to say, boundaried spaces are nothing more than "mind-stuff." At this level, consequently, the boundaried space for $\sqrt{-1}$, or of a unicorn, deserves the same status as the boundaried space of a "horse," and the boundaried space of a dream the same status as a "real world" space. In this sense, a human's range of "real world," fictive, imaginary, and dreamed spaces is enormous. He has open to him, at every moment, many alternatives. In contrast, the lower organism's range of possible spaces at a given moment is severely limited. This is because, as we shall observe below, it is a "radical dogmatist"—its world must be either one way or the other.

One chief reason for the human's increased freedom is that he possesses a tremendous capacity for naming, for using natural language to represent boundaried spaces. Naming potentially establishes the chasm between what is "real" and what is a representation of the "real" (i.e., not really "real"). What can be conceived as not really "real" implies the prior construction of abstract sets of boundaried spaces corresponding only partly to the physical world. And such abstract boundaried spaces, revealed in everyday language use, in art, in science, in fantasy and dream, are the product of the imaginative mind which, as we shall also observe, is potentially capable of infinite variability. Hence:

COROLLARY II: *To name a boundaried space is to name an abstract form, not a content.*

Let us now see how distinct boundaried spaces constructed by members of the same or of different communities partly vary, and at the same time, partly coincide.

2.16 *The act of naming is always perspectival.* Furthermore, it is invariably indeterminate and it differs from any and all alternative perspectives. Consider for example a triangle:

Figure 2

We may agree that it is a triangle. But it can be other things depending upon the perspective and the context. Wittgenstein (1953, 200e) tells us that it "can be seen as a triangular hole, as a solid, as a geometrical drawing, as standing on its base, as hanging from its apex; as a mountain, as a wedge, as an arrow or pointer, as an overturned object which is meant to stand on the shorter side of the right angle, as a half parallelogram, and as various other things." In addition, in a primitive society it might be the omniscient eye of god. To the schizophrenic it might be a pointed instrument that threatens to kill him. And so on.

A name tends to force us into seeing the manifestation of a boundaried space in a particular way. Nevertheless, every name that is attached to the manifestation of a boundaried space can be contrasted with some other incommensurable perspective and with some other name that might possibly have been used but was not. A name represents, through the mediation of a boundaried space, a given aspect of the world or a purely imaginary entity. But to attach a name to a boundaried space and to assume invariance with respect to the object, act, event, or imaginary entity which that name represents is to fail to take into account the infinity of additional potentially or actually significant qualities and properties that might otherwise be attributed to that object, act, event, or imaginary entity from other perspectives. Hence associated with any name there is *incompleteness* and *indeterminacy*—as well as arbitrariness. In spite of this the name is a necessary entity; true at least for a given time in a given place and for a given individual or group of individuals. However, no name can lead to the possession of an absolute form of knowledge with respect to a represented object, act, or event that is totally free of perspectivism and potential error.

2.17 To illustrate the inexorable perspectival nature of all knowledge, consider this:

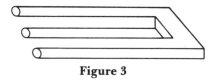

Figure 3

"It is paradoxical," you say. But, of course, it appears paradoxical precisely because you strive to perceive an orderly and noncontradictory universe from within your Western world conceptual framework. And you generally assume that you can ultimately describe this universe in terms of Cartesian "clear and distinct ideas." If we show the same drawing to an Australian aborigine, perhaps, unlike us, he would not be accustomed to projecting three-dimensionality onto two-dimensional planes. Perhaps he would tell us: "It's a bunch of lines on paper, there's nothing more to it." Perhaps, unlike Plato's ingenious slave boy, he would not be able to intuit such supposedly universal essences as "circularity," "rectangularity," "cylindricality," etc.

2.18 Now let us consider a further "thought experiment" concerning the incommensurability of perspectives. What if we enclose Figure 3 within two overlapping boundaried spaces, like a Venn diagram?

The portion of the object inside A possesses a "circular" motif, the portion inside B has a "rectangular" motif. The two aspects of the drawing are contradictory (incommensurable) because, at some point along the prongs, "circularity" becomes "rectangularity" or vice versa; there can be no "square circles" in our "rational" world: A ∩ B is by itself noncontradictory, but within the context of the whole drawing it presents a contradiction. That is, A ∩ B is part of two continuous ("analog") wholes that contradict each other and at the same time it is itself noncontradictory and a continuous whole. Since A and B, two

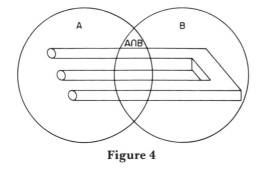

Figure 4

continuous wholes, are mutually contradictory, a "digital" switch is required in order to go from one to the other; this is because they possess incommensurable modes of organization. At the same time, A ∩ B represents the transition between A and B although A ∩ B is not a "digital" entity: It is also an "analog" continuum.

I submit that this simple diagram is the graphic illustration of a universal phenomenon: *Particular perspectives, self-sufficient and consistent from within, are, to a degree, inevitably contradictory with respect to other perspectives or to larger contexts.* Therefore, as was implied above, we are all endowed with certain inborn perceptual as well as conceptual faculties (Popper, 1972). There will always be a degree of "overlap" between meanings of words, concepts, and entire world views held by members of distinct communities—and hence they will be able at least partly to communicate. At the same time, language-bound, culture-bound, and world-view-bound imperatives will render these communities partly incommensurable—and consequently they will never be able to communicate clearly and distinctly with one another (in this light I refer once again to F. A. Hanson's excellent 1979 article).

Examples:

(a) Two children, one from Colorado and the other from Indiana, can speak about "mountains," believing at the outset that they are communicating. Yet only up to a certain point do they understand each other. The first child's "mountain" rises sharply four to five thousand feet above the valley floor; that of the second is a round-topped mound no more than a few hundred feet high. The first "mountain," sometimes seen from a distance, can be blue in color, and it is usually snow-capped; but to call the second blue would ordinarily seem absurd, for it is never seen at a distance. And so on. There is continuity as well as incommensurability between the two meanings of the word "mountain."

(b) A European missionary remarks to some African pygmies, when the trail they are walking along leads into a grassy area, that the mountains in the distance are gorgeous. He communicates nothing to them since, for survival purposes in this jungle habitat, their perception ordinarily need not reach more than a few hundred yards, and hence they have no name for "mountains," nor do they differentiate the darker blue patch along the horizon from the lighter blue of the sky above. Yet the missionary can, with some degree of adequacy, explain to them what a "mountain" is by analogy to the small hills in their immediate vicinity.

In both cases communication breaks down due to the degree of incommensurability between meanings and/or concepts—that is, between the inner boundaried spaces they construct. Yet communication can and does occur within the "overlapping" area where there is a degree of consensus, sometimes most effectively by analogy. Moreover, the "overlapping" zone is compatible with each of the two incommensurables, yet transformation from one to the other requires a "digital" leap. That is, "mountain" (Indiana) must be transformed into "mountain" (Colorado)—a radical meaning (and boundaried space) switch—or "hill" must be, by analogy, transformed into "mountain"— a radical concept (as well as boundaried space and name) switch. Such switches obviously occur, enabling us to communicate, with varying degrees of effectiveness. At some level, then, universals must exist, though they have not yet been clearly specified. At this universal level, what we see and what we say is made possible by the human capacity to generate relatively complex systems of abstract conceptual boundaried spaces. Yet the variations, from culture to culture, and from past to present to future, are astounding in their complexity. How can we better account for this variability, which, we must suppose, is virtually unknown in animal communication?

Let us begin at the first step toward answering this question by seeing the world through the frog's eye.

2.19 A frog "does not seem to see or, at any rate, is not concerned with the detail of stationary parts of the world around him. He will starve to death surrounded by food if it is not moving. His choice of food is determined only by size and movement. He will leap to capture any object the size of an insect or worm, provided it moves like one" (McCulloch, 1965, 231). But the frog is not inherently so stupid as it might appear. The fault lies not in its brain but in its eye. For the eye "speaks to the brain in a language already highly organized and interpreted, instead of transmitting some more or less accurate copy of the distribution of light on the receptors" (McCulloch, 1965, 251). That is to say, the frog's eye abstracts from the physical world, and consequently what the brain "sees" is the result of what has been abstracted a priori.

The frog does not "see" the same world we do. Its eyes do not move; if the frog's body changes position its entire vision is changed with it. It has no fovea, or region of greatest acuity upon which it can center part of its vision. It has only a single visual system; its retina is uniform throughout. The frog's vision is specifically adapted for detecting dark objects that are smaller than its receptive field and that enter the field, perhaps stop, and move about intermittently; the ideal system "for detecting an accessible bug" (McCulloch, 1965, 254). However, the frog's eye limits its perception of discontinuity due to this generally broad continuous perception of the world.

2.110 In contrast to the frog, we humans are capable under certain conditions of altering our perspective at will in order to perceive discontinuity-contradiction-incommensurability. We can oscillate from figure to ground, from the Gestalt diagram of juxtaposed faces to the vase, or from "circularity" to "rectangularity" in Figure 4. That is, we are capable of "seeing" two or more perspectives from "above." By extension, it can be stated that with respect to our world view, our conceptual frameworks, and our total cosmology, the world we "see" is a world that with varying degrees of difficulty could be "seen" otherwise.

Consider, in this light, the world of the "Flatlanders" or the "Line-landers" marvelously described by Abbott (1952). Their perception was inexorably limited to the number of dimensions within which their world was constructed. However, though with great difficulty, a "Linelander" was able to conceptualize a two-dimensional world and a "Flatlander" a three-dimensional world. Similarly, our own world view is slowly incorporating the notion of a four-dimensional space-time manifold, which, given sufficient time, might well become part of our commonsense notions (for further discussion, see Merrell, 1980b, Chapter Four).

Recent work on perception—the "Ames room" and other similar

phenomena, Gregory's (1966, 1970) work on the "intelligent eye," Arnheim's (1969) and Gombrich's (1960) studies on the perception of art, Hall's (1976) studies on cultural variability, Goodman's (1978) pluralistic universe, and perhaps even Whorf's (1956) hypothesis of linguistic determinism—demonstrate that our "real world" is bound to a particular set of conventional perspectives. And that "real world" could always have been something other than what it is. What is the relationship between these conclusions and the above discussion of the frog's perception?[5]

The frog's construction of a boundaried space, a "bug," as the case may be, is determinate. It is determinate because what the frog "sees" is limited to what its eye lets it see, and it is, we would suppose, incapable of "seeing" something other than what its eye is physiologically equipped to detect. Perception for humans, in contrast, is potentially infinitely variable. There are, of course, certain limitations to what we can "see." These limitations are tied to our innate biological capacity for perception. Nevertheless, at another level there exists for us the possibility of a potentially limitless number of perspectives ranging from public and culture-bound modes to those that are private and idiosyncratic.[6] Given this possibility, we incessantly generate boundaried spaces at biological, cultural, and individual levels, and with each successive level greater parameters of freedom are enjoyed. Therefore:

PROPOSITION I: *The number of distinct perspectives and their accompanying boundaried spaces that humans are capable of constructing is potentially unlimited.*[7]

Now for a preliminary illustration of how this virtually limitless construction of boundaried spaces can be accomplished.

2.20 Additional "Thought Experiments"

2.21 With your face about two feet above a light smooth surface, close your right eye and fix the gaze of your left eye on a particular point on the surface. Place a small coin at that point and begin moving it slowly to the left. When the coin is inside your "blind spot" you will no longer be able to see it. It has disappeared into a dark "hole," although you of course know that it is still there on the smooth continuous surface. Now quickly take away the coin, and, if you have not removed your gaze from that point you will discover that the smooth surface has "reconstructed itself." The discontinuous "hole" has disappeared and you once again perceive a smooth continuum! The conclusion: It is possible to "see" what is there simply because we "know-believe" that it is supposed to be there (see Peirce, 1960, 5.220).

2.22 In the sciences it has also been possible to "see" what is there because the scientist wants it to be (or knows that it is) there.

Mark off a boundaried space from the unboundaried: ☐. Call the space a "quark," Q: ☐⌣Q. Replace Q by the boundaried space: ☐☐. The boundaried space followed by the boundaried space is the same as the boundaried space: ☐☐ = ☐. Quarks have been created-invented.[8]

Now, assume that quarks have not yet been named. Cross over into the imaginary space in which they can potentially exist, and then recross it. This is the same as not crossing it at all: ⟦/⟧ = ____. Quarks therefore remain a potential not yet actualized.

Or do they? If, according to the above formulation, the boundaried space has been recrossed, it is "negated" to produce the unboundaried. However, with respect to boundaried spaces created-invented by the human mind, memory traces remain throughout time. Words and boundaried spaces cannot simply be categorically erased from the mind. Furthermore, if these words and boundaried spaces are "written" they will not only have a temporal dimension, as in memory traces, but they will now possess an objective material and spatial dimension as well.

The "logical" Axioms I and II pertain appropriately and exclusively to an atemporal dimension. However, when introducing temporality all boundaried spaces and their corresponding names (that is, all signs) must be considered in terms of their relations to all other signs in the Peircean sense. To "negate" a boundaried space by recrossing it is to negate only the "spatial" aspect of the sign. Such "negation" does not simply leave a "hole," at least where the time-bound human organism is concerned, for this "hole" is necessarily "filled" with "something," and this "something" is necessarily something that follows in time and is to a greater or lesser degree something other than the original boundaried space.

Hence that exact boundaried space no longer exists, but neither has it been merely "negated" or "annihilated." It has become another *difference*. To conceive/perceive *difference* is, at the local level, to be aware of discontinuities within continuous wholes. At the global level it is to be aware of discontinuity-contradiction-incommensurability between otherwise continuous wholes (that is, between distinct perspectives) such as was the case of the "circular" and "rectangular" organization in Figure 4. Now, it is obvious that *differences,* or two distinct perspectives, cannot be conceived/perceived simultaneously. A minimal unit of time must transpire between one concept/percept and another concept/percept. It is imperative, then, that from this point onward in this inquiry we must work toward a consideration of temporality. Proper inclusion of temporality in the model being constructed is necessary since, following from PROPOSITION I, the construction of a potentially unlimited number of boundaried spaces from a potentially unlimited number of perspectives is, given human limitations, only possible over an unlimited extension of time.

In order to begin the first step, a few more preliminary "thought experiments" will illustrate in a metaphorical and graphic way how discontinuity arises out of continuity or vice versa.

2.23 Construct a Möbius strip by taking a strip of paper and connecting the top corner of one end with the bottom corner of the other end. You now have this:

Figure 5

The strip encloses a space, a boundaried but "warped" space. Traveling along one surface (boundary) of the strip (enclosed space) you can go continuously from "inside" to "outside" without removing your finger from the surface (boundary) of the strip (enclosing a space). Recall that the name and the boundaried space named ordinarily combine to form a sign that is like two inseparable wholes. However, along the continuous Möbius strip such a discontinuity between space and name is "transcended" since one side of the surface can suddenly become the other side, and vice versa.

What is the meaning of this? The "warp" in the strip is "like" names that are fused and (con)fused with the boundaried spaces they name. The name may be mistaken for the boundaried space, or the boundaried space may be mistaken for the content of the name when in fact a different boundaried space was intended to be the representation of the name. And so on. To consciously create a metaphor also entails such a "warp" or (con)fusion. Conversely, at nonconscious levels, to interpret a metaphorical name literally or a literal name metaphorically is to (con)fuse name and boundaried space without knowing it. In essence what occurs is that, like running your finger along the surface (boundary) of the Möbius strip, a discontinuous "switch" is (consciously or nonconsciously) perceived in what would otherwise be a continuum.[9]

The Möbius strip is a two-dimensional plane "warped" through three-dimensional space. Actually we are required, in order to illustrate such a "warp" in our conceptual space, a three-dimensional object interjected into the fourth dimension. This, however, will be wellnigh impossible, since four-dimensional objects are not properly imaginable. Let us try the next best procedure, then, with an indirect illustration.

2.24 Construct a "Klein bottle" by taking an infinitely pliable elongated balloon, cutting a hole in the side and another one in the bottom of the same diameter as the opening of the balloon, and putting the neck of the balloon through the first hole and sealing it to the circumference of the second hole. This is a cross-section of what you now have:

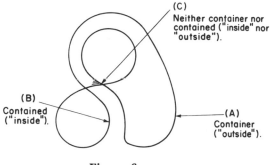

Figure 6

(B) is part of (A) and at the same time it is contained within (A). In contrast, (C) is neither contained within (A) nor is it part of (A). (C) is different from both (A) and (B). Yet it connects (A) to (B), both of which ordinarily represent two incommensurable and contradictory entities. That is, (C) is itself, like A ∩ B in Figure 4, describable as a continuity that connects two entities that are discontinuous-contradictory with respect to one another. Transition from (A) to (B) is possible only by an all-or-nothing "digital leap" or "catastrophe."[10] Yet this "leap" or "catastrophe" occurs along an "analog" more-or-less continuum and at a point where one level of organization abruptly becomes another.

2.25 A continuous space that connects two discontinuous-contradictory spaces along a general continuum can be found in all culturallybased human conceptual frameworks (Douglas, 1966, 1973; Leach, 1964, 1976). Consider, say, the concept of human sacrifice. The victim must carry a petition from man to the gods. But it is impossible for him to exist in their presence since, as an ordinary human being, he is unclean, mortal, finite, etc., and hence exists in a realm that is contradictory to that of the gods who are without sin, immortal, infinite, etc. The victim must be transformed. Through a set of rituals he becomes "like" the gods while at the same time he exists with ordinary men, and he is therefore capable of existing with the gods while at the same time he is "like" all men. In essence he is neither man nor god but both man and god "simul-taneously." Now, this is a contradictory situation, and thus the victim must be immediately sacrificed, for walking contradictions in an otherwise orderly cultural system are strictly prohibited! This phe-nomenon can be constructed along the lines of the Venn diagram (compare to Figure 4):

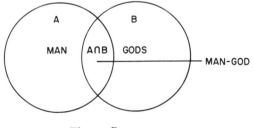

Figure 7

All cultural taboos and prohibitions tend to follow this general pattern where the overlapping or "fuzzy" areas are avoided. Such taboos and prohibitions are erected on cultural and on idiosyn-cratic levels with the intent of providing a noncontradictory, or-derly, balanced, symmetrical world. However, novel ideas and creative works of art also play directly on the "fuzzy" areas. It is in these "fuzzy" areas where, like the transition from "inside" to "outside" along the surface (boundary) of the Möbius strip or the Klein bottle, new metaphors are created and new perspectives are invented by means of a recategorization of that orderly, balanced, symmetrical cultural world.

For instance, consider metaphorization. In order that a "man" be metaphorically equated to a "fox," there must be a set of contradictory attributes possessed by both (i.e., biped/quadruped, hairless/furry, etc.) and another shared set of attributes, within the "overlapping" area (i.e., sly, cunning, swift, etc.). (See Merrell, 1980b, 1980c, for further discussion.) "Sly," in this metaphorical context, takes on two meanings: One meaning "humanizes" the fox (and hence it means what it would ordinarily not mean in reference to a human) and the other meaning "animalizes" the human (and hence it means what it would ordinarily not mean outside the metaphorical context). "Sly," of course, exists in the "overlapping" area, A ∩ B, but each of its two meanings pertains to the larger areas, A and B, which are, outside that "overlap," incommensurable.

Now consider an exceedingly more complex level of conceptualization: the transition from the Newtonian to the Einsteinian world view. The key word here is "simultaneity," which in the Newtonian framework is made possible by the supposed infinite speed of light, and which according to Einsteinian relativity can never exist for two observers, since the speed of light is finite. The same word has different meanings in two chiefly incommensurable frameworks. Yet, as is well-known, an altered meaning of the word allowed Einstein a loophole outside the Newtonian framework. "Simultaneity," in other words, existed in A ∩ B; it was the "warp" affording entry into another world; it projected a discontinuity into what would ordinarily be conceived as a continuity.

In sum, we often fail to realize the important role that our knowledge and beliefs play in our recognition of objects, acts, events, and meanings of words because of our familiarity with them insofar as they are related to our everyday life. We often fail also because much of this knowledge and these beliefs was acquired through unreflective and tacit processes—i.e., like learning to walk or talk as a child, or to ride a bicycle or play tennis some years later (see Polanyi, 1958). Yet the information we read from our environment is, it must be admitted, actually both complex and subtle. And at any given moment we can be consciously aware of only a minute part of it. Nevertheless, over time and by breaching ordinarily discontinuous boundaries, we can become aware of a phenomenal array of novel objects, acts, events, and meanings.

Hence:

PROPOSITION II: *Culture dictates a determined set of boundaried conceptual spaces. Individuals perpetually resist these cultural injunctives by breaching boundaries and creating new frames in order to conceive/perceive discontinuities where continuities were supposed to exist, and vice versa.*

This notion of a perpetual rupture of boundaries and the creation of frames is a necessary condition for the possibility of conceiving/perceiving, over time, a potentially unlimited number of boundaried spaces and perspectives as put forth in PROPOSITION I.

Chapter 3
Steps toward the Mediation of Contradictory Spaces

3.10 Preliminaries

3.11 In the first part of this chapter I will propose a primitive mechanism with which to specify: (1) the cultural-collective mediation of contradictions by the conception/perception of continuity in what might otherwise be discontinuity (Figure 7), and (2) what lies at the roots of individual acts of bringing about change in culturally dictated boundaried spaces by conceiving/perceiving new discontinuities and continuities. I believe these steps are necessary to set the proper foundations for an epistemology of written texts, for we must adequately account for: (1) the fact that meanings of texts, given altering contexts, undergo changes, and (2) the process by which the meaning of one's world can undergo change, even though slight, through the reading of a text.

3.12 Let us begin this time at another beginning: the rudiments of metaphor and paradox.

Consider two dogs in a fight. Many signs are present: growls, barks, showing of fangs, bristling hair, snaps, etc. The larger dog soon has the advantage over the smaller dog. The smaller dog suddenly stops growling, barking, snapping, showing fangs, bristling, etc., and exposes its defenseless underside. The larger dog, rather than "finishing off" the smaller dog, trots over to a tree some distance away and urinates on the trunk, then leaves. The small dog "invited" the large dog to attack, but this sign did not denote what it would ordinarily denote. Things worked in the opposite way.

Let growls, barks, fangs, etc., be represented by a boundaried space: ◯. This space denotes "fight."

Let the unprotected belly of the smaller dog be represented by the opposite boundaried space: $-$◯. This space denotes "not-fight." (Since each space is a holistic icon there can be no negations in the sense of language or logic.) Combining the spaces produces no space, the unboundaried. Hence: ◯ $+$ $\left(-◯\right)$ $=$ _____. The fight has been "nullified." Notice that this is the same as crossing the boundary into the boundaried space and then recrossing it.

3.13 Now observe two dogs engaged in play activity. They nip rather than bite each other (see Bateson, 1972, and Wilden, 1972, for earlier discussion of this phenomenon). The nip constitutes a boundaried space that is part of a larger boundaried space, the bite. The bite denotes the equivalent of "This is war," while the nip denotes the equivalent of "This is play." This situation is unlike that of the two dogs engaged in a fight. In the preceding case the small dog created a boundaried space representing the opposite of what would ordinarily be created in fight activity. Consequently, the boundaried space denoting the equivalent of "This is war" was "nullified." Now, however, the message denoting "This is play" is part of the message denoting "This is war." Hence part of one boundaried space (nip) does not denote what the whole boundaried space (bite) would ordinarily denote. Moreover, war activity is in essence similar to play activity. What is the meaning of all this?

Let nip-bite be a primordial sort of *code,* and let the equivalent of "This is play" and "This is war" be *messages* generated by this code.

Since the nip is part of the bite, call the nip-bite relation *metonymy,* and since play activity is similar to war activity, call this relation *metaphor.*

Let nip and bite be represented by boundaried spaces: nip $=$ ⬭ bite $=$ ⓑ . Let space *a* stand in relation to "play" and space *b* stand in relation to "war" in the same way that in 1.32 *x* stands to the circular boundaried space.

To use *a* is to convey a message that means something other than but yet something similar to what it would ordinarily mean. In this sense a message conveyed by *a* is "fictitious" or "metaphorical." The receiver of the message must be aware that it is meant to be interpreted figuratively rather than literally. But confusion can and does arise. Dog *p* nips dog *q*—part for whole—which denotes the equiva-

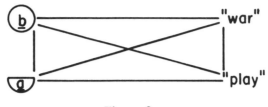

Figure 8

lent of play activity, which is analogous to war activity. Dog *q* interprets the message "as if" it were really the real thing. A fight ensues, perhaps until one animal marks off a boundaried space that denotes the opposite of those boundaried spaces denoting war activity. If this occurs the two dogs may subsequently resume their play activity.

The dogs are incapable of communicating explicitly about nips and bites, yet they engage in a rudimentary form of metacommunication insofar as the distinction between play activity and war activity is made by a more-or-less variation of the same message and insofar as the context surrounding the activity in which the two animals are engaged to a major degree determines how the message will be interpreted.

Since one sign can constitute part of another sign in the same code, and when using that sign it must therefore refer to itself but on distinct levels, the nip-bite system entails essentially a paradoxical situation. War activity and play activity, although similar in a metaphorical sense, represent two incompatible wholes at distinct levels. In contrast, nips and bites that create messages within these two activities exist at the same level of organization. Graphically these relations may be illustrated by the following:

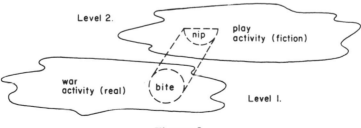

Figure 9

Signs generated by the code consist of a continuous "analog": more-or-less pressure by the clamping down of teeth. In contrast, the messages and concomitant activities represent two discontinuous and incommensurable systems. On moving from one level to the other a "digital leap" is required, like the Gestalt switch from figure to ground or vice versa in the well-known faces-and-vase diagram. Notice that the code is a more-or-less affair while the activities are either-or affairs. Notice also the similarity between Figure 9 and the Venn diagram in Figure 4. In other words, the "clamping down of the teeth" is like the "overlap" in the Venn diagram which, though continuous, represents a potential discontinuity between two partly incommensurable domains. More appropriately, this nip-bite system demonstrates that a leap from one domain to another partly incommensurable domain is made possible by "metaphor," by the continuum. And since when metaphors are erroneously taken literally they are contradictory if not meaningless, it becomes clear that to jump out of a given domain and into another incommensurable domain involves what would ordinarily be perceived to be irrational or contradictory.

3.14 The preceding section entails what might be called "code switching." It demonstrates that, at the most fundamental level, animal forms of communication contain the rudiments of human creative activity. In order to illustrate this further, consider the well-known "liar paradox." To say "All Cretans are liars," or "That Cretan is a liar," is noncontradictory. On the other hand, "All Cretans are liars said the man from Crete," is a contradictory and even paradoxical statement since it refers back to itself. The Cretan (individual man) makes a statement about all Cretans (a class of men) within the same frame. The statement is true if and only if it is false and it is false if and only if it is true. It creates a paradoxical situation. Notice how the relationship between an individual man and a class of men is part to whole (and more-or-less) as is the continuous nip and bite, and that the act of lying is an all-or-nothing discontinuous affair like play activity and war activity. Notice also that when the Cretan paradox doubles back upon itself there is "code switching" whereby the sentence must be viewed now as true, now as false, ad infinitum.

Obviously the rudimentary metacommunicative canine system described above possesses some of the basic properties of "code switching" that exists in human languages, although of course there is no syntax in it (Sebeok, 1972). The reason members of the canine family and other animals with such primitive metacommunicative systems do not become as confused and "schizophrenic" as humans is most likely because they are incapable consciously of moving to higher metalevels. However, it has been demonstrated that humanlike anxieties occur in, for instance, the dog that cannot distinguish between an oval and a circle as they are gradually made to appear more and more alike. This would be similar to the imaginary case of one dog whose nip threshold is relatively "hard" and another animal whose bite threshold is relatively "soft." Perplexity may ensue when they try to communicate.[1]

3.15 Recent studies with "talking apes" shed more light on the possible origins of "code switching" and language and conceptual change.[2] In the absence of the proper phonological apparatus with which to generate speech patterns, chimps have been taught to use a form of sign language, or to "speak" by placing magnetized plastic tokens of different shapes on a board, or to write "sentences" on a typewriter connected to a computer. These chimps may have occasionally and spontaneously demonstrated a certain degree of creativity that bears similarity with the nonspontaneous nip-bite phenomenon.

I will mention only a few cases. A watch has been referred to by one of these chimps as a "listen," a smell in the kitchen has been called a "flower," and "cry hurt food" has been attached to radishes. Note that in each case there is a continuous metonymical relationship established between auditory, olfactory, or gustatory properties, and objects possessing those properties. Note also that in other instances such as when a cat is called a "dog," or "nonspeaking" chimps are called "black bugs," metaphorical relations of similarity between ordinarily discontinuous classes of things are established. Some form of awareness of classes and class relationships is further substantiated by a chimp's ability to classify an object it has never before seen, such as an orange, into abstract categories by calling it a "ball," "fruit," or an "orange-thing."

The ability to abstract is not limited to human cognitive capacity. It is possessed to a degree by animals. This by no means verifies that the chimps are capable of using language with humanlike adequacy even though, in addition to their being creative, they do "speak" with a rather primitive form of "syntax." Neither does it indicate that the difference between animal and human powers of abstraction is simply a matter of degree rather than kind. There is in reality a type distinction between human abstraction and animal abstraction that will be the focus of a later section.

Hence, for the moment, a proposition that logically follows from PROPOSITION II:

PROPOSITION III: *At the primitive level of signaling activity (such as the nip-bite phenomenon), boundaried spaces potentially undergo change: Discontinuities potentially become continuities and vice versa.*

3.16 In light of the above and in addition to the 1–1, 1-2a, 1-2b, 1-2c, and 2-1 relations proposed for the hierarchy in 1.29, we can now add the following:

(f) 2-2 RELATIONS. At the metonymical-metaphorical level, one of a pair of possible messages can induce one of a pair of possible responses (nip-bite, and play activity).

(g) 1-N RELATIONS. A single input can result in N number of outputs that are determined by laws of association of abstract categories, classes, and types (possibly the "talking apes," humans).

(h) 2-N RELATIONS. Two different inputs (i.e., a sign and an index, a sign and a symbol, an index and a symbol, etc.) can induce N number of outputs (possibly the "talking apes," humans).

(i) N-N RELATIONS. N number of inputs can give rise to N number of possible outputs (specifically humans at conscious levels). (This entails open systems of multiple relations governed not only by biological, but also, as will be observed below, by culture-bound, world-view-bound, and idiosyncratic conceptual frameworks, beliefs, and modes of perception.)[3]

(i) involves human consciousness of past and future such that messages can be displaced over broad ranges of time and space; they no longer need to be tied to the immediate situation. With respect to the language from which these messages are derived, it also allows for reconstitution. That is to say, by a process of analysis messages are treated not only as inviolate continuous wholes but are broken down into smaller discontinuous and arbitrary parts, and by a complementary process of synthesis those smaller parts can be rearranged into a potentially infinite range of other messages that in their totality are perceived and conceived as continuous wholes.

The possibility of N–N relations also entails not only culture-bound and world-view-bound "language games" and the activities implied by them, but also the possibility of a relatively sophisticated level of metacommunication about these "games" (see Ruesch and Bateson, 1951; Watzlawick, Beavin and Jackson, 1967; Watzlawick, Weakland and Fisch, 1974). Hence, a given system, relatively simple or relatively complex, can be conceived/perceived as a set of orderly, balanced, and symmetrical signs. From a metaperspective, however, apparent contradictions can arise in the system by the construction of new categories and modes of conception/perception.[4]

In order to illustrate the potentially infinite number of possibilities implied by the N–N relations, I will digress for a moment to offer some additional "thought experiments."

3.20 Where Do New Perceptual Modes and Conceptual Frameworks Come From?

3.21 Consider this rather simplistic "universe of possible discourse" (see also Merrell, 1976a, 1980a):

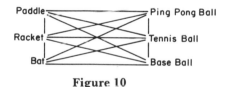

Figure 10

Each left-handed item in the figure is related to its corresponding right-handed item by contiguity. The words and relations between the words are in the beginning arbitrary in the Saussurean sense. Horizontal lines connect contiguous terms corresponding to a particular "game" that is conceived/perceived as a continuous "analog" whole. Vertical lines connect analogous terms existing in "games" that are discontinuous with respect to one another. And diagonal lines connect a term existing in one "game" with another nonanalogous but contiguous term from a different "game."

In this way, for instance, paddle-racket-bat, or ping pong ball-tennis ball-baseball, arbitrary with respect to their own isolated domain, can now be integrated into the total system such that the analogous relations between them become necessary, rather than arbitrary. Baseball-bat are arbitrary terms at the sign level within a respective "game." On the other hand, baseball-paddle are related nonarbitrarily by the simultaneous lines of analogy (baseball-ping pong ball), of contiguity (ping pong ball-paddle), and of nonanalogy (baseball-paddle). However, there exists an analogy *in potentia* between terms connected by diagonal lines.

3.22 For example, I bring out a bat and a ping pong ball and declare: "Let's play ball." I have apparently confused what would otherwise be discontinuous boundaries between "games." It seems that I have interpreted objects (boundaried spaces) from two different systems as contiguous objects (boundaried spaces) within a system. Like the schizophrenic, I have construed as real what would ordinarily not be the case. My mind has evidently been "warped," as in the Möbius strip model, such that I have (con)fused boundaried spaces and names. This temporarily places you in a difficult position. Which "game" do I intend to play and which rules should we follow? First you might doubt my knowledge of the possible "games" in the system, or you might become skeptical and cease to believe that I am serious. Then you might attempt to clarify the situation and reply: "This is for playing ping pong and that is for playing baseball. Now, the difference between the two 'games' is as follows: . . ." When you finish, I, by this time exasperated, remark: "You don't understand. What I want to play is base-pong ball. Now, the rules of this 'game' are as follows: . . ." What are we doing? Communicating on different levels. First, boundaries were confused, then lines of comparison and contrast were established, and finally disquisition about the "games" and potential creation of a new "game" took place. The upper levels involved metacommunication, and only through metacommunication could the apparently contradictory situation be resolved. Now it was possible for new lines of analogy, contiguity, and nonanalogy to be established with the concomitant creation of a new "game" and new rules.

3.23 Compare these "game" systems to the nip-bite phenomenon as illustrated in Figure 8. The construction of two metaphorical activities (war and play) from a metonymical code (nip-bite) potentially creates continuity from what otherwise would be discontinuity (i.e., like Figure 7). However, when the hypothetical "schizophrenic" dog interprets a "hard" nip as a bite, discontinuity is perceived where continuity would ordinarily exist. The nip-for-play connection is sanctioned by social imperatives (undoubtedly biologically based in this case). But the nip-for-war connection is most probably, at least in the beginning, the product of some sort of "idiosyncratic" or "individual" act. And this act marks the potential beginning of some new form of activity.

With respect to the "games" and by means of extended metacommunication based on the Figure 10 system, two ordinarily nonanalogous but contiguous items (boundaried spaces) from two different (discontinuous) "games" can become conceived/perceived as contiguous parts of a whole new (continuous analog) "game." Subsequently, at the metacommunicative level this new "game" can potentially become part of our cultural conventions. This is as if the "schizophrenic" dog were able suddenly to create and institute, by explicit metacommunication with other dogs, a new form of canine activity as a result of its original (con)fusion of a message. However, the dog is obviously not capable of such extended metacommunication. And, were we to communicate only by nips and bites, our metatalk would have been equally impossible.

3.24 In addition, the uniquely human level of N-N relations described above entails "involuntary" and "irrational" acts of belief, suspension of disbelief, doubt, skepticism, suspicion, intention, hope, etc. Consider the following imperatives:

(a) Go fetch that stick.

(b) Get me a glass of water.

(c) Be spontaneous.

(d) Believe in God!

I can easily train a dog to carry out (a), and perhaps even a chimp to obey (b), but (c) and (d)? Is the difference between the first two and the last two not that the former are "voluntary" while the latter are "involuntary"? That is only part of the answer. Commands (a) and (b) stand for physical actions while (c) and (d) do not. The former refer to action on the external world of things while the latter refer to dispositions that can potentially result in physical action on the world. In fact, the recipient of commands (c) and (d) is placed in an untenable position. He cannot voluntarily obey what ordinarily pertains only to involuntary control. How can a child obey, for instance, (c)? If he is spontaneous he cannot willingly obey the command, and if he attempts willingly to obey it he cannot at the same time be spontaneous. He is placed in a quandary.

This quandary resulting from command (c) presupposes the ability to make a self-referential statement such as, "I am spontaneous." If the speaker is spontaneously emitting the utterance it is true. But if he is spontaneously uttering it he cannot simultaneously and consciously speak about its quality of spontaneity; hence it is not true: a contradiction. Similarly, command (d) presupposes a statement like, " 'I know' I believe in God." When the speaker says he knows he believes, he is speaking about his belief; but in so doing he cannot simultaneously be acting on the basis of or from within his belief. On the other hand, when he acts on the basis of or from within his belief he acts "as if" he knows, but he cannot simultaneously and consciously say what it is that he knows. That is, he cannot at the same time talk about his belief. He must do either one or the other but he cannot do both at the same time.

Belief, doubt, and skepticism, etc., then, somehow entail ordinarily nonconscious levels of action stemming from embedded dispositions. On the other hand, speaking about them entails a distinct, and non-simultaneous, level of activity. The task now at hand is to show how these two nonsimultaneous levels of consciousness can give rise to the potentially infinite variety of N-N relations described above. This is a necessary step, since: (1) disquisition about texts or about a specific text entails the construction of a metatext, and (2) as is intuitively obvious, the number of written texts, past, present, and potentially future, represents an infinite number of possible combinations.

3.30 Where Do Belief, Doubt, Skepticism, etc., Come From?

3.31 Consider a hypothetical case: the conversion of person x from his religion to another, supposedly incommensurable, faith (see also Merrell, 1980c).

x's religion is for him a continuous whole, and it is discontinuous-contradictory-incommensurable with respect to any and all other religions. x is told by a well-meaning missionary, y, that he must "suspend his disbelief" in order to accept the truthfulness of y's faith. By this request it appears at the outset that x can simply unsuspend suspension of disbelief in his own religion (R_1) and then proceed to suspend disbelief in the new faith (R_2) and passively receive it. However, the problem is that, at this almost instantaneous moment, he must be "suspended," in a form of "limbo," between R_1 and R_2. He cannot be still inside R_1 for, if so, he could not at the same time have suspended disbelief in R_2. And he cannot be properly inside R_2 for, if so, his transference of belief would be an accomplished fact. He would possess no "free agency" to choose between R_1 and R_2 after unsuspending disbelief in one and suspending disbelief in the other. But he must be either in R_1 or R_2 or in some larger continuous whole, a sort of "metaperspectival framework," which exists outside both R_1 and R_2.[5] If he believes either in R_1 or R_2 he of course believes in something. If, at the split moment after he unsuspends his suspension of disbelief in R_1 and before he suspends disbelief in R_2, he exists in this "metaperspectival framework," it still cannot be said that he believes in "nothing." Even to believe in such a "nothing," if indeed the postulated "metaperspectival framework" is considered to be "nothing," would be in itself a belief in "something" not necessarily actual but at least potential. x is not and cannot be at any time in no framework. Total absence of any framework or perspective can only be the equivalent of death.

To unsuspend disbelief in R_1 is to admit to the possible truth value of either R_1 or R_2, or something else in the possible realm of the continuous "metaperspectival framework." When x almost instantaneously places himself in the "metaperspectival framework" by assuming that either R_1 or R_2 is possibly true, he is simultaneously opening himself to a potentially infinite range of specific possibilities. To deny all of them except R_1 and R_2 is eventually to place himself either inside R_1 or R_2, and he is in the process led to believe in one or the other. Naturally, if y is an effective evangelizer x will undoubtedly be led in the direction of R_2. Yet while x is momentarily inside the "metaperspectival framework" the fact remains that any number of possibilities might be before him.

It nevertheless appears that x can, "in a flash," comprehend the "truthfulness" of R_2. If x is indeed converted, he will of course possess no recollection of any "metaperspectival framework." But this does not prove that it is not "real." Recall, for example, that the "hole" in the table during the experiment in 2.21 was part of our "real" perception. Yet we ordinarily filled in the gap in order to make the table appear continuous. We were ordinarily not aware of the "real hole" in our perceptual faculties!

By extension, if from the "metaperspectival framework" a potentially infinite number of possibilities exists, then all imaginary entities, whether or not they correspond to the world as it is conceived and perceived, must derive from that source. To select (abstract from the "metaperspectival framework") a finite number of these entities at a given moment is to construct a new world or to reconstruct a part of the old world. In this process discontinuities are made continuous and continuities become discontinuous. *Differences* are generated.

Hence: The infinitely extensible framework of metaperspectival boundaried spaces is coequal with dream reality, poetic free flights of imagination, mystical religious experiences, scientific creativity, and all "analogical" acts, be they of minor or major proportions (cf. 2.14).

3.32 What I am suggesting is radical. It is commonly accepted that normal experiences can and do occur in dreams, poetry, mystical experiences, etc., but to claim that any and all dreams and poetical and mystical experiences can and in many cases have come to be considered normal experience is an unorthodox position. In this sense, one of all possible worlds can at a given time and place become *The World* (Melhuish, 1973). It follows that what is commonly accepted as "normal," "logical," or "rational" was once part of that infinite realm of all possible worlds. And what we commonly accept as "normal," "logical," or "rational" might not be so in another culture at another time.

3.33 To be "inside" a belief is to be part of a set of tacitly held conventions and modes of behavior. It is to "know" how to "see" and to do things generally without having to think about them. It is to "see" and do them ordinarily without speculating on the possibility that there might be other viable ways of "seeing" and doing them. To be "converted" to another religion or to another "form of life" one must step "outside" this circle, in order to exist momentarily in that realm where there are other alternatives, potentially an infinite number of alternatives.

This metalevel perspective I speak of will have a bearing on propositions put forth at a more advanced stage of this inquiry. However, for the moment we must return to the level of spaces, names, and their representation in order to consider more specifically the nature of language change, which is of utmost importance when inquiring into the underlying reality of written texts. Then, in Chapter 5, we will return to the all-important consideration of time, without which the potentially infinite variability of texts would be impossible, before discussing in further detail the nature of the written sign.

Chapter 4
When Are Boundaried Spaces Real?

4.10 Metaphor: When Things Are Not What They Ordinarily Would Be

4.11 The task is now to show, from the level of animal perception to human conception/perception, how metaphor and metonymy entail three important aspects of the sign activity outlined above: opposition, negation, and *differentiation*.

4.12 Paralyze a dozen or so bugs, put them in the box, and place a frog in the box with them. Observe that the frog will not (cannot) eat the bugs, so remove it before it starves. The stationary bugs represent part of the frog's whole perception of "bugness." It is physiologically equipped to "see" only the whole, not the immobile parts. That is, the parts (the immobile "spots") are meaningless if they are not in motion. Consequently, so to speak, it "cannot see the forest for the trees."

Let me illustrate the frog's problem with a similar human problem. Once a man was shown the various buildings, gardens, points of interest, and so on at an institute of higher learning. At the end of the tour he remarked: "Yes, but where is the University?" It was explained to him that the various buildings were all part of the University; that the former were material constructions and the latter an abstract category. The perplexed man had committed a "category mistake," confusing ordinarily incompatible levels of abstraction (Ryle, 1949).

As far as the frog is concerned, dark spots plus movement equals "bugness." Among paralyzed bugs it "perceives" only dark "spots"—

the part for the whole. The frog sees stationary dark spots without realizing that they possess the necessary qualities to be potentially perceived as members of a general class of things. In a comparable way, the naive man saw only buildings housing certain functions without realizing that they were part of the whole he wanted to perceive, or, a child may see in the trees nothing but trees, unaware that these trees are members of the general class of things making up an abstract entity called forest.

Pavlov's dog and the "talking apes" have manifested the same phenomena, although it must be remembered that their behavior is, we would assume, biologically motivated to a greater extent than human social and individual behavior.

4.13 Consider the converse of the above examples wherein a "category mistake" on a rather trivial scale is consciously brought about. If, in using metonymy, I intentionally say "crown" for "king," "wheels" for "car," or "pad" for "apartment," I am using words ordinarily denoting parts of wholes to denote the wholes. Similarly, when the dog "nips" it sends part of the whole message to denote an activity other than what would ordinarily be denoted by the whole message. But if the other dog interprets it as the whole message the unintended activity will follow; the second dog has also committed a sort of "nonconscious category mistake." Hence boundaried spaces can consciously or nonconsciously be (con)fused in the part-whole hierarchy and at distinct levels of abstraction.

4.14 Now on a similar scale consider metaphor, which in many cases is a form of "category mistake" wherein something is perceived to be in some sense new and other than what it would ordinarily be perceived as. At the most fundamental level, certain caterpillars have developed a large dark spot behind their head that appears to be a monstrous "eye." It seems, at least to us humans, that the most obvious "purpose" of this ingenious sign is to frighten predators. In other words, this icon represents a message something like: "Beware, I'm mean": a natural scarecrow. If successful it deceives its enemy by means of metaphorically denoting something other than what the succulent morsel would otherwise denote. That is, the enemy constructs the boundaried space "danger" rather than the ordinary boundaried space "lunch time." However, the caterpillar's behavior is inherited and "unintentional." We would assume that it is totally unaware of the "purpose" of its metaphorical icon of deceit.

4.15 Yet the caterpillar illustrates a very important point. All forms of metaphorization always have a negative aspect: They relate two entities that are not conventionally compatible in the ordinary mode of signification (negation has already been discussed at the root level of animal communication in 1.27-28). A metaphor presents something as not being what it would ordinarily be, of denoting something it would ordinarily not denote. In essence, then, being aware of a metaphor-as-metaphor calls attention to what ordinarily would not be the case (Hausman, 1975). Conversely, nonconsciousness of the metaphor-as-metaphor entails perception of what ordinarily would not be the case as what really is. The metaphor in this instance becomes part of the real world.

The caterpillar's message is, we might suppose: "I am not your lunch; I am ferocious." It fulfills the negative characteristic of all metaphorization, but this beast must carry its metaphor around with it whether it wants to or not because it is the metaphor and the metaphor is its real self. In contrast, when the opossum says, "I am not alive," or when the bird whose offspring are threatened sends out the message, "My wing is not healthy," negation is "intentional" and real—although the "intention" is in these cases biologically triggered and hence probably equally inherited. The messages just described exist at a primitive and nonconscious level of "metacommunication." That is, the demonstrated sign that conveys a message that would not otherwise be the case is automatically a message about that absence of what would ordinarily be a presence.

With respect to humans, on the other hand, to consciously and intentionally send a message about what would ordinarily be present but is in reality absent is in a basic sense like a caricature of, say, Winston Churchill depicted as a bulldog. The cartoon evokes the message: "Churchill is not human; he is metaphorically a bulldog because he possesses bulldoggish attributes. But at the same time this bulldog is not what would ordinarily be a bulldog, because it possesses human attributes."[1] However, in this case, unlike the previous examples of animal communication, the degree of freedom allowed when the cartoonist draws the caricature is phenomenal. Adequate conciousness of the metaphor-as-metaphor entails the transcendence of some ordinary culture-bound mode of classification (the creation of discontinuities from what would otherwise be continuities). Then this metaphor can be understood and transmitted in culture by explicitly formulated means or by implicit example and imitation. It bears mentioning that this conscious level of metaphorical creation cannot occur without the "metaperspectival framework" described in 3.31.

4.16 Metaphors also exist at broad cosmological levels: "root metaphors" or "paradigms" (i.e., primarily in myth, religion, science, and metaphysics) (see Kuhn, 1970; MacCormac, 1967; Pepper, 1942). Moreover, these broad-based cosmological metaphors can for the human organism become so embedded that, like the relatively nonconscious animal or the human committing a "category mistake," there is no longer any awareness of the original "purpose" of the metaphor (see also Merrell, 1980b).

Consider how a metaphor of the most general kind can be generated consciously in the beginning only later to become embedded in consciousness to effect language-bound and world-view-bound modes of perception. For example, Descartes speculated in his *Discourse on Method* that:

> I have described the earth and the whole visible universe *as if it were* a machine, having regard only to the shape and movement of its parts (quoted in Turbayne, 1962, 39).

Descartes' "machine metaphor" over the centuries has generally become ingrained in our thought processes so that it has come to be tacitly assumed that the universe does not operate "as if" it were a machine; it "is" in reality a machine (see von Bertalanffy, 1967; Koestler, 1971; Turbayne, 1962; Whitehead, 1948, for example). Of course, the general "schizophrenic" tendency of all human beings to occasionally mistake a metaphor for the real thing or vice versa is well known. Here, in a similar way, I am speaking of the embedment of a metaphor in the scientific view of the universe, which has had a marked effect on the Western world mind. The "machine metaphor" has become a boundaried space that is no longer properly perceived as a metaphorical boundaried space. It is assumed to be simply the way things are. It is as if, like the Möbius strip, our minds had become "warped" by the distorted image of the metaphor without our possessing consciousness of the "warp." Or, like the caterpillar, it is as if we were not conscious of the original "purpose" of the metaphor, for we now automatically perceive it to be natural rather than as something other than what it would ordinarily be.[2]

4.17 Among the more intelligent animals as well as humans, a certain confusion or "category mistaking" is also entailed in play activity.

It is generally conceded that human play is goalless, chiefly gratui-tous, uncertain, and unproductive, yet many times regulated and make-believe (i.e., it is composed of metaphors and fictions) (see Caillois, 1969; Ehrmann, 1971; Huizinga, 1955). The same can be said of play among the higher nonhuman primates. Play among these primates always consists in mock fighting, eating, copulating, etc. That is, it is an activity denoting what it would ordinarily not denote in the sense of a metaphor (Hockett and Ascher, 1964). There are among the nonhuman primates certain code-switching messages which elicit play activity. These messages are always directed toward a specific animal. For example, to induce a play chase a monkey "may approach another animal by walking or trotting towards him with a highly characteristic bounce to the gait; the head bobs up and down, his gaze may not be directed at the animal he approaches, he is often wearing the play-face and soft gutteral exhalations may be audible. . . . As he reaches the animal he is approaching and gains his attention he turns around and makes off at a slow lolloping pace in the opposite direction, looking back over his shoulder to see if the other animal is following. His head is still bobbing, he is still wearing the play-face" (Loizos, 1969; see also Sebeok, 1972; Simonds, 1974). This activity, before it can become play, must transform the animal's behavior from one set of response patterns to another: "code switching" (Altmann, 1962).

It appears most evident that play activity is equally shared by hu-mans and animals in the case of porpoises that have "taught" humans to do tricks. Under certain conditions, these mammals have found, if they toss a rubber ring to someone standing at the rail, "that person will quickly learn to throw it back, and will continue the game until the porpoise tires of it. That two creatures of such unlike habit have learned to share an activity that yields mutual enjoyment speaks well, I think, for both porpoise and man" (Wood, 1954).

4.18 Hence, with respect to all human and nonhuman forms of play activity, two sets of messages are necessary (a) to initiate play, by means of "code switching," and (b) to reinforce the "idea" that "this is play" by a pattern of codes that is different from the nonplay codes (Simonds, 1974). The first, by its imitative nature, generates the idea that the activity is in a metaphorical sense not really what it would ordinarily be, and the second must, at the metacommunicative level, maintain a distinction between what figuratively is and what ordinar-ily would really be.

In a general sense, then, play activity involves the metaphorical-like perception of an alternative "world" whose sign structure is like the cosmological "machine metaphor" described above. That is, for instance, the dogs' messages, which might conceivably be something like, "This play is a fight," is analogous to Descartes' stating, "This universe is a machine." Yet, of course, to properly interpret the metaphor or the play activity demands some form of awareness that the universe is not really a machine, or concomitantly, that the play is not really a fight. If not, confusion may arise.

Therefore, it becomes apparent, from this summary discussion of play, that:

PROPOSITION IV: *The negative characteristic of all levels of metaphorization is induced through "code switching."* (Basically the same can be said for metonymy, where the part is not really the whole and therefore it denotes what it ordinarily would not denote.)

This "code switching" in PROPOSITION IV can explain how, from PROPOSITION III, "boundaried spaces potentially undergo change" when "discontinuities potentially become continuities, and vice versa." That is, the transition from one coded level to another requires a "digital switch."

4.20 What Kind of Mental Representation Must Metaphorical, Metonymical, or "Real" Boundaried Spaces Have?

4.21 The problem situation at the level of human perception is now this: Must boundaried spaces, "real" or figurative, necessarily *be*, in the eye, or in the "mind's eye," or do they not necessarily need to be "imagined" at all. If the latter is the case purely conceptual boundaried spaces can *be* for which there are no visualizable images. In this sense the potentially unlimited number of boundaried spaces and perspectives over time, as put forth in the above propositions, becomes feasible.

4.22 As was pointed out in 2.13, it is easy enough to imagine a unicorn even though one does not exist in the physical world. This is because the whole unicorn is constructed from ordinarily incompatible parts of whole entities that exist in the physical world. Even though the class of things that ordinarily have horns or a horn is breached (discontinuous parts separated from a continuous whole), there appears to be no real paradox here, only a simple "category mistake."

Now see if you can conjure up the image of a "square circle." Although squares and circles are incompatible entities, it might seem that we should be able to combine them in order to produce a new visualizable fictitious entity. Why cannot this be done? Perhaps, one might argue, it is because squares and circles do not exist in the real physical world, only things that are square or circular. However, try to imagine a "cubical basketball." Is this not an easier task? But, it might be said, this image is not really contradictory since a basketball is round merely by cultural convention, and the convention can easily be altered by our intentionally changing the shape of the "ball" and consequently also the rules of the game. The apparent anomaly therefore presents no long-term conflict.

However, imagine a "cow-horse." What would it look like? At the outset, at least, this appears to be as much a contradiction as a "square circle," for we do not know which parts of the cow and which parts of the horse to combine—except possibly in Russian, where the word for "cow" originally meant "horn." Here we have words that denote ordinarily incompatible things in the real world, not words that denote nonreal geometrical objects that we arbitrarily fabricate for the "games" we play and that are governed by equally arbitrary rules. But you say that it is possible to imagine a "cow-horse" by arbitrarily deciding on which parts of each animal to combine and make a unique whole animal. However, if we do this we have created a fictitious animal that reasonably should have a different name attached to it, perhaps "corse." If this is the case, could we not just as easily take part of a square and part of a circle to make a whole "square-circle," perhaps called a "squircle"? Here, of course, we would do violence to Platonic eternal forms; but then, it might be that concepts are "invented" by the creative mind rather than "discovered." If this is so, perhaps there is actually no limit to the possible number of creative constructs of which we are capable.

4.23 However, let's try imagining in terms of quantity. It is relatively easy to picture in the mind a sack containing 10, 50, 100, or 200 potatoes. But 100,000 potatoes? Difficult but still possible. What about an infinite number of potatoes in a sack? Or even 1,000,000,000th of an infinite number? Impossible. I assume that we believe in the "reality" of infinity, yet it is unimaginable and unfathomable. Does this, however, subtract from its "reality"? Does infinity or even $\sqrt{-1}$ possess a more or a less legitimate form of "reality" than a unicorn, a centaur, a Pegasus, or even a "squircle"? The mere fact that a conceptual entity has no material referent or even that it cannot be properly imagined does not necessarily render it absolutely and eternally "irreal" (cf. note 1, Chapter 2).

For example, Sterne's Tristram Shandy once began to write his autobiography in minute detail. After one day's labor he discovered that he had compiled only one-half a day of his life. Perplexity mounted. He would never be able to finish, for if he wrote an infinite number of days, half of those days would not be included in his book. But the book would be infinite, since half of infinity is infinity, therefore his task should be terminated. But how could it be, if in his writing he is destined to fall further and further behind? Here we have an "unimaginable" problem. But does that mean that it is not "real"? Is it any less real than such "unimaginable" questions taken seriously as: the number of angels that can dance on a pin, the function of phlogiston, or the mythical "aether" through which light is propagated, or even an Einsteinian four-dimensional space-time continuum?

4.24 To repeat, modern physics demonstrates that current models of the ultimate nature of the world can be formulated mathematically even though it is not possible to construct a mental picture of these models nor can natural language adequately describe them. These purely hypothetical constructs have in many cases come to be accepted as valid models with which to describe the real world. Yet it is impossible to escape the premonition that what is ordinarily regarded as "real" is in reality no more than a set of self-referential conceptual boundaried spaces and names for those boundaried spaces. And since boundaried spaces and names are considered to be something other than the physical world to which they refer, then they are necessarily the expression of something other than that physical world. They become, like Peirce's signs, "an endless series of representations, each representing the one behind it . . . [which becomes] nothing but the representation itself conceived as stripped of irrelevant clothing. But this clothing never can be completely stripped off; it is only changed for something more diaphanous. So there is an infinite regression here" (Peirce, 1960, 1.339; see Merrell, 1979, for discussion of the compatibility between Peircean thought and modern physics).

In this sense it might be said that we try to know more so we can see more, and hence we create more signs that refer to other signs in our attempt to explain all signs and ultimately to explain the world.

But this is also ultimately a problem since, as recent studies in psychology demonstrate, we generally "see" what we "know" and "expect" we will "see." That is, our signs become for us *The World* we (believe we) perceive. This circle is not necessarily vicious, however, for in the purely conceptual realm ever new boundaried spaces and names can be and are created to form new signs. And these signs at the outset need have no necessary and direct correspondence to the physical world: They refer only to other signs.

4.25 In the purely conceptual realm (or what in 3.31 I call the "metaperspectival framework") it is possible to create "mental" constructs ranging from imaginables to purely formal unimaginables. But what is in the beginning pure form may become imaginable as thought and natural language evolve, when the "correct language" has been found with which to speak adequately about new situations (see Bridgman, 1958; Heisenberg, 1958; Capek, 1961). This conceptual realm can be considered as nothing short of infinite in extension. The history of creative ideas in the arts, science, and elsewhere attest to the fact that whether gratuitous or practical, there is no end to the number of conceptual and even perceptual possibilities. This must certainly be the case, for otherwise how could such diversity exist in the way members of distinct human cultures conceive and perceive the world? The existence of primitive thought, Oriental philosophy, meditations of mystics, the knowledge explosion in Western world science, artistic creation, etc., can only lead to the conclusion that there exists potentially an infinite array of distinct conceptions and perceptions of the world.

On these brief comments I rest my case, for the moment at least. I believe we will agree that it is the only premise upon which a hypothesis of unlimited conceptual and perceptual change over an unlimited period of time can be formulated. In the next chapter I will propose an "imaginary" model with which to account for the possibility of the creation, over time, of alternative, and potentially contradictory or even incommensurable, imaginary and purely formal constructs. This, I submit, is a necessary step, since written texts constitute the most noteworthy embodiment of such constructs.

Chapter 5
Toward a Model for the Generation of Time: A Digression

5.10 Preliminaries

5.11 Begin at another beginning where signs, the union of boundaried spaces and names, have already been given an ontological reality by a human being or a collective group of human beings.

COROLLARY III: *Signs are perceived through two modes: "digital" or sequential and "analog" or parallel. The first, in the broadest sense of the term, may be called metonymical, the second metaphorical* (see also Merrell, 1976b, 1978a, 1980a, 1980c).

This corollary follows from developments in Chapter 3.

5.12 Recall that to construct a boundaried space and then to construct it again is the same as constructing it. Recall also that to cross the boundary and then to cross it again is the same as not having crossed it. Now we have these operations:

(1) ◯◯ → ◯.

(2) ⊘ → ____.

And if we reverse the direction of the arrow:

(3) ◯ → ◯◯.

(4) ____ → ⊘ (see Spencer-Brown, 1969).

Call (1) and (2) *contractions*. Call (3) and (4) *expansions*.

5.13 Metaphor is contraction. To say that a man is (metaphorically) a lion, a sound is (metaphorically) high, or a color is (metaphorically) cold, is figuratively to reduce the two terms in each case to the same boundaried space. But since they cannot "logically" be the same boundaried space there is no mere substitution of man for lion, high for sound, or cold for color; these metaphorically equated boundaried spaces exist in a state of "interaction." That is, they "interact" with one another in such a manner that they are conceived/perceived in a novel way that would have been impossible had they remained in isolation (see, for instance, Berggren, 1962/63; Black, 1962; Mac-Cormac, 1976; McCloskey, 1964; and for discussion of these views, see Leatherdale, 1974). On so combining they must "interact," since, given the negation inevitably in all metaphorization, that which is explicitly negated must be implicitly present, for otherwise the metaphor would be construed as literal rather than figurative.

For example, I state that: "The lion (metaphor for man) is growling." The name of that "man" is absent but at the same time implicit, while "lion" as the name of the boundaried space is explicit. Concomitantly, the boundaried space, which would ordinarily represent that particular "man," has been altered by the metaphorical interaction between that "man" and "the class of all lions" such that it now represents something other than what it would ordinarily represent (see Merrell, 1980c).

Hence the act of metaphorization artificially *contracts* two ordinarily unequal boundaried spaces into one: $\bigcirc\bigcirc \to \bigcirc$. And it does this by recrossing one boundaried space such that it is "negated," although it remains implicit in the interactive interpretation of the metaphor: $\varnothing \to \underline{\hspace{2em}}$.

5.14 Metonymy is expansion. The metonymical use of "wheels" for "car," "cup" for "cup of tea," or one part of speech for a whole utterance (i.e., "Get," for "Get me the newspaper") renders implicit a word or expression, which would otherwise be explicit. "Wheels" is explicit, but since it is part of the "car" it does not alter figuratively the implied boundaried space representing the "car." In this sense "wheels," "car," and their representative boundaried spaces can coexist, one being explicit and the other remaining implicit. In addition, metonymy depicts a relative level of "analyticity" since what would ordinarily be the whole image is broken down into smaller constituent parts. This characteristic contrasts metonymy with metaphor, which is relatively "synthetic" since it rearranges interacting (but otherwise incompatible) wholes to form a larger figurative whole (see also Merrell, 1980c).

Hence the act of metonymization *expands* what would ordinarily be one boundaried space into two: $\bigcirc \to \bigcirc\bigcirc$. But at the same time it entails the presence of a space that would ordinarily not be used but that is crossed and recrossed in order to make possible the construction of the boundaried space implied by the metonymical term. Hence: _____ → $\emptyset$.

5.15 In general, metaphor is a *contraction* of explicitness that implies an *expansion* of tacitness. Comprehension of a metaphor implies tacit awareness of increasingly larger wholes and the interactions between them. In contrast, metonymy is an *expansion* of explicitness accompanied by a *contraction* of tacitness. Awareness of constituent units and their interactions within wholes is required. This might appear strange. Nevertheless, general tacit awareness of a boundaried conceptual space presupposes subsidiary tacit awareness of the structure, properties, and functions of the parts making up that space. This broad level of awareness enables one to relate a given space to other actual and potential spaces. On the other hand, explicit awareness of the parts of a boundaried space makes it possible to relate the properties and functions of these parts of the whole, but the inner shell of that space is not penetrated. In other words, the "wheels-car" relationship remains "inside" while the "man-lion" interaction relates across otherwise incompatible boundaried spaces whose "overlap" allows for points of similarity between them—i.e., brave, fierce, aggressive, etc.

The same characteristic of metonymy applies to contiguous words in strings as it does to boundaried spaces (Jakobson, 1960; Jakobson and Halle, 1956). Comprehension of a proposition as a whole does not necessarily require focus on each of its specific parts, and consequently the proposition, as a compounded boundaried space, can be juxtaposed and compared with other propositions. In contrast, focus, metonymically, on particular linguistic units making up that proposition in general isolates it, at least for the moment, from all other propositions (see Neisser, 1967; the notion of compounded propositions will be taken up in Chapter 9).

5.16 The next question is this: How is it that apparently, and over an exceedingly small increment of time, we can relate boundaried spaces to one another from "without," such as in the case of metaphorization, while somehow "simultaneously" maintaining awareness of those spaces from "within," as in metonymization? That is, how can we prevent a boundaried space from being simply "negated" or effaced when replaced in consciousness by another space to which the first is to be related? In other words, what is an implicit (tacit) space such that we may know it?

First, consider this "thought experiment": Say to a nonspeaker of Spanish: "Voy a casa." It is to him incomprehensible, a series of meaningless sounds. He cannot establish any meaningful relationship between these sounds uttered by another human being speaking a foreign tongue and the meanings and signs in his own language that he has internalized. The beginning student of Spanish, on the other hand, may with a little difficulty decode the message. "It means, 'I'm going home' " he tells us. It is to him "meaningful," "sensible," and "logical." Now say to him, in the context of a conversation involving male-female relationships: "Me dio calabazas"—which literally translated is, "She gave me squash," but it is a colloquial expression equivalent also to, "She two-timed me." "It is 'nonsensical' and 'meaningless' " he remarks. He cannot establish any correlates between the utterance and what he has thus far learned in Spanish, or between the utterance and a meaningful translation into his own tongue.

A fluent speaker of Spanish as a second language, on the other hand, has internalized a greater portion of this second language system. Consequently, "Me dio calabazas," is "nonsensical" and "meaningless" when translated literally into his native tongue, but he does not ordinarily consider the utterance to be meaningless since he can immediately establish meaningful positive and negative correlates between the two languages. In addition, the utterance is meaningful to him because he can relate it to his repertoire of lexical items and the grammar rules in this second language. Hence he also understands the utterance within its own system because he has learned to "think in Spanish." However, when he "thinks in Spanish" he cannot simultaneously establish the correlates between the two languages. But when he establishes the necessary correlates between the Spanish utterance and its equivalent in his own language, he cannot simultaneously "think in Spanish." Each activity involves a distinct level, and a "digital switch" is required when moving from one to the other. At one level, a statement in a language may be meaningful from within its own framework. At another level the statement becomes meaningful by virtue of the correlates (translation) between that language and another one. This second level is the metalevel. (Compare this phenomenon to the "metaperspectival framework" described in 3.31.)

The upshot of this "thought experiment" is that, where perception and conception are concerned, there are no simultaneities. Like the Gestalt "switching" from above examples, perception and conception must remain either in one domain or in another contradictory or incommensurable domain, but not in both at precisely the same instant in time, except possibly from a higher level perspective. Consequently, if one boundaried space is explicit in consciousness, and another implicit, the implicit space can be recalled to consciousness and the explicit space made implicit. But if the two spaces are ordinarily incompatible, they are not, in exact simultaneity, capable of being compounded into one space at the same level. Something must be either relegated to the background or, according to the above "thought experiment," the incompatible spaces can be incorporated into a higher metalevel.

5.17 However, although we cannot be simultaneously "inside" and "outside" word strings or clusters of boundaried spaces, the fact remains that we do indeed function "as if" we were. That is, we obviously tend to believe that we can be both "inside" and "outside" in simultaneity, although logically and physiologically speaking, I have conjectured that we cannot. How can this conjecture be accounted for? I will attempt to demonstrate how by means of an "oscillatory" model of the nature of thought processes.

Currently it is believed that all "reality" is of a "pulsating" nature. In the 1920s de Broglie proposed that particles of subatomic matter should display a wave-particle duality. A later extension of de Broglie's ideas by Schrödinger reduced this matter to a set of mathematical functions describing wave patterns. Subsequent and increasingly complex mathematical formalization of nuclear physics ultimately gave rise to the question: What are the waves of wave mechanics waves of? Some hoped that it would soon be discovered that these waves had some tangible embodiment in the physical world, but to no avail. It appears that subatomic particles can either be formally described as waves or they can be detected as particles, but each activity entails a perspective that is contradictory with respect to the other. Moreover, when focus rests specifically on the corpuscular nature of a subatomic particle its wave is unspecifiable, or when the position of a particle is specified its velocity is unpredictable—this is a rough definition of Heisenberg's indeterminacy principle.

Today it appears that the physicist, like the Oriental sage, is unable to draw a precise line between particle and wave, matter and energy, being and nonbeing, or time and space (Capra, 1975). In light of this observation, allow me to suggest that to be properly intelligible, boundaried spaces must be viewed as inseparable from their signs, content as inseparable from expression, and meanings as inseparable from marks. To focus exclusively and specifically on spaces, content, or meanings is to render unintelligible and unspecifiable their complementary signs, expressions, and marks. These entities compose an inseparable whole that can be adequately comprehended only by attending to it synthetically in partly tacit and partly conscious ways. Moreover, these entities composing this whole constantly interact, incessantly changing themselves into the other. Everything, from subnuclear particles upward, oscillates between itself and other, existence and nonexistence. You cannot step in the same river twice.[1]

5.18 Following Peirce's notion that thoughts possess sign characteristics, and from the idea that external signs are the material manifestation of boundaried spaces (or thoughts), why cannot it be said that thought is, like the ultimate nature of matter-energy, oscillatory?[2] Notice that for the mind to function when thinking as if it were simultaneously "inside" and "outside" a boundaried space (or thought) is necessarily an illusion since, considering that a boundaried space is in essence an "analog" whole, there must be a "digital leap" when entering and leaving it. Hence to be "inside" and "outside" it implies the coexistence of continuity and discontinuity: a contradiction. However, with an oscillatory model this becomes intermittantly possible. In 2.22 I discussed the impossibility of boundaried spaces being "negated" absolutely since, in human beings at least, memory traces cannot be totally erased. Somehow a discontinuous space perceived at a given instant is connected to another discontinuous space perceived at another instant to create an (actual or illusory) continuous whole. The model I want to propose for describing this phenomenon can be illustrated (albeit unavoidably rather vaguely) by means of the "Klein bottle" wherein discontinuity exists within continuity:

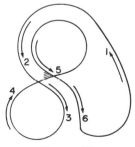

Figure 11

If we move along either surface of the "bottle" there are transformations according to Table I.

1	CONTINUITY	INSIDE CONTAINER (= IMAGE)
2	RUPTURE OF CONTINUITY BY "CATASTROPHE"	NOT CONTAINER AND NOT CONTAINED
3	CONTINUITY	INSIDE CONTAINED (= BOUNDARIED SPACE OR CONTENT)
4	CONTINUITY	SWITCH TO OUTSIDE CONTAINER (= IMAGE)
5	RUPTURE OF CONTINUITY BY "CATASTROPHE"	NOT CONTAINER AND NOT CONTAINED
6	CONTINUITY	OUTSIDE CONTAINED (= BOUNDARIED SPACE OR CONTENT)
1	CONTINUITY	SWITCH TO INSIDE CONTAINER (= IMAGE)

Table I

This oscillation provides the same "picture" as the following wave pattern:

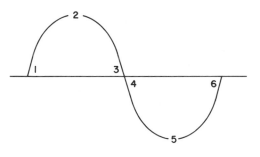

Figure 12

This model requires that the wave be what is known as a "traveling wave," characteristic of waves on water. Another wave characteristic, called a "standing wave," can be produced when two "traveling" waves of the same amplitude and wavelength move in opposite directions along the same plane such that there is no resultant horizontal motion. "Standing" waves can be produced in a rope tied to a stationary object. There exists a wave form but it does not advance; the waves simply move "up and down" (see Figure 13). Such "standing waves" are believed to be the type of wave motion of the electrons at various energy levels in the atom.

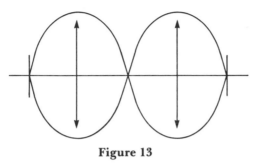

Figure 13

5.19 Consider a hypothetical situation with respect to "standing waves." We have a resonant chamber full of air that can be insulated from its surroundings in such a way that, unlike a bell or a musical instrument, it loses no energy. Assuming ideal conditions, we can store energy in it indefinitely by causing it to resonate at a frequency at which one wavelength terminates exactly at the wall of the container, so that the rebounding wave produces with the oncoming wave a "standing wave." Now the chamber can, by taking up energy of the same frequency from its environment, progressively build up energy at that frequency while all other frequencies are canceled out (see Figure 14). Notice that this process occurs within a closed system. There is input but no output. Compare this process to the oscillations in Figure 15 and Table II.

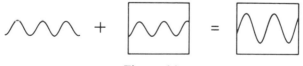

Figure 14

The equivalent "standing wave" pattern is depicted in Figure 16. Notice that the first "bottle" model represents oscillation between "outside" and "inside" like "traveling waves," while the second "bottle" represents oscillation from "within," like "standing waves." Notice also that the second is symmetrical and reflexive or self-reflexive with respect to boundaried spaces, names, and signs. This is because the

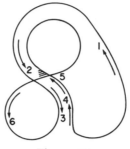

Figure 15

1	CONTINUITY	INSIDE CONTAINER (= IMAGE)
2	RUPTURE OF CONTINUITY BY "CATASTROPHE"	NOT CONTAINER AND NOT CONTAINED
3	CONTINUITY	INSIDE CONTAINED (= BOUNDARIED SPACE OR CONTENT)
4	IDENTICAL TO 3 BUT THE INVERSE (MIRROR) IMAGE	
5	IDENTICAL TO 2 BUT THE TRANSITION TO/FROM THE INVERSE (MIRROR) IMAGE	
6	IDENTICAL TO 1 BUT THE INVERSE (MIRROR) IMAGE	

Table II

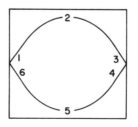

Figure 16

first enjoys "extrinsic reference" while "reference" for the second is "intrinsic"; it "refers" to itself and can therefore constitute a metalevel of discourse. It follows that the second can pertain to purely conceptual or imaginary states where, like "squircles," "corses," and "unicorns," there exist no referents in the world.

5.110 Now it might appear that according to this model, intrinsic and purely conceptual or imaginary boundaried spaces, like the "standing wave" model, manifest no "transmission through space." In contrast, the extrinsic oscillatory pattern "travels through space" from "inside" to "outside" referent and back again. However, the situation is not what it seems. In reality, signs (boundaried spaces plus names) are labels that specify what might be called "space-time events." And signs can function only insofar as they are somehow anchored in these events. The question is: How?

Both the "standing wave" model and the "traveling wave" model are necessarily time-bound, and their function is manifested by means of spatial coordinates. Just as we cannot simultaneously perceive both figure and ground or faces and vase in the Gestalt drawings, just as x could not unsuspend disbelief in R_1 and suspend disbelief in R_2 at the same instant, just as one cannot be "inside" the Spanish language and at the same time translate Spanish into English from "outside," or just as signs cannot be perceived both from the "digital" (metonymical) and "analog" (metaphorical) modes, so direct internal linkage of boundaried spaces to names and indirect external linkage between signs and objects, acts, and events in the world cannot occur in simultaneity. Some "unit of time," although extremely small, must transpire during the transition from one mode to the other, so to speak, "through space."[3] The union of this "unit of time" and this transition "through space" constitute what is perceived as an indivisible "space-time event." In this sense, what we think of as time can be defined as merely the temporal oscillation of conception/perception through some imaginary space from "inside" to "outside," or from container (image) to contained (concept). Or, if you will, time can be considered merely a function of our brain-wave rate (see, for example, the speculations of Bentov, 1977; McKenna and McKenna, 1975; Floyd, 1974).[4]

This notion is intimately connected to what is known as Zeno's paradox, which can equally be resolved in terms of "space-time events." For example, if our awareness in the present, the here and now, occurs only during an exceedingly small increment of time, and if we could somehow remain exclusively "inside" that increment, then as Zeno proclaimed, movement would be logically impossible. A photograph of a race car in action snapped at a few thousandths of a second produces a frozen image of a machine. This image is like the "snapshot" our mind receives many times per second. Yet we are unable to perceive the timeless and separate still shots, interpreting them through time as a smooth flowing stream of "space-time events."[5] This is necessarily the case, since all units of our conscious experience overlap.

Here is an example. Construct a row of equidistant dots on a cash-register tape. Let a rod long enough to cover three dots represent our conscious experience. If we slide the rod along the lines, at each "instant" we are at a here and now, but it is tinged, to paraphrase Whitehead, with mediate memory of the past coupled with anticipation of the future.[6]

It follows that since we must be able to relate a given oscillation "outside" the space or sign to a previous oscillation, or since we must be able to relate an "up and down" oscillation of the internal wave pattern to its inverse, then there must be some notion of the accumulation of "space-time events." That is, we must have memory. Moreover, when purely imaginary and spatial fictions such as "demons," "martians," "mesons," "pions," "quarks," or perhaps even "corses" are directly or indirectly "seen" in the world, this memory must have made them part of our external perception of temporality. That is, the illusion is formed of a temporal and physical framework for what in the beginning was purely imaginary (spatial).

5.111 Now, how is it that new and "real" items in one's "real world," new metaphors or metonyms, or during rare moments, totally new "worlds" can be derived from one's imaginary items of experience that originally did not correspond directly to that "real world"? Reconsider the act of x's conversion from one religion (R_1) to another (R_2).

Let S_1 be the state of suspension of disbelief in R_1 and S_2 be the state of suspension of disbelief in R_2. This second religion at the outset can correspond to x's world only in a make-believe or imaginary sense; it is not yet "real." The task is to describe how for x it can become "real" and how x can become conscious of his consciousness of its "real" nature.

Let the original state plus the agent, x, be: $(S_1 - x_1)$, and the final state after conversion be: $(S_2 - x_2)$. Let p be the probability of x's remaining within S_1, and q be the probability of his being converted and passing into S_2. Now, at a given point x unsuspends suspension of disbelief in R_1, and if he is properly converted, he "simultaneously" suspends disbelief in R_2. If not he will re-suspend disbelief in R_1. It can be stated that with probability q he will do the former and with probability p he will do the latter. Assume that at this "instantaneous" moment when the transition is to occur, we can ask x whether or not he intends to be converted. The set of possible responses he will give us can be defined as: $[p\,(S_1-x_1) + q\,(S_2-x_2)]$. All this appears to be logically satisfactory. While x "instantaneously" resides in the state of "limbo," neither in S_1 nor S_2, we can assume that he is capable of deciding between the alternatives before him.

However, assume that we can ask x a few thousandths of a second after he responded to our question: "What did you believe you would do when we asked you whether you intended to be converted or not?" And, assume that he answers: "I already told you, I intended (did not intend) to be converted." His intentions were already "in" his mind when we asked him the question. He was tacitly aware of what he intended to do and of the world he wanted to "see" and to believe in without yet possessing immediate consciousness of his intentions. Then after our second question he could, by "introspection," become mediately and explicitly aware of what his intentions were. But at the same instant it would have been impossible for him both to have the intention and possess immediate and explicit consciousness of that intention—this phenomenon pertains equally to all nonvoluntary acts and states of being such as conversion, belief, doubt, skepticism, etc. (see Merrell, 1980b; also Wigner, 1970, from which this "thought experiment" was derived).

Hence, while in the "metaperspectival framework," x possessed at least some sort of tacit awareness of the possibility of (S_9-x_2) as well as of (S_1-x_1). Yet he was not consciously "outside" (S_1-x_1) and not yet "inside" (S_2-x_2). Therefore, he must also have possessed some tacit sort of consciousness of the potential states, that is, of the "mixed states," (S_1-x_2) and (S_2-x_1). x's not-so-conscious consciousness at the point of "conversion" while within the "metaperspectival framework" was now actually a state of suspension of all disbelief, a sort of suspended animation. At that precise moment his consciousness could be none other than a coequality with all consciousness, a tacit awareness of many possibilities of belief. If this notion is to be accepted, it follows that x's condition, while in such a metastate, can only be defined as: $[(S_1-x_1) \wedge (S_2-x_1) \wedge (S_1-x_2) \wedge (S_2-x_2)]$. That is, discontinuous space-time events are combined to form a continuous whole. However, *consciousness of this whole is possible only after the fact.* Only in retrospect, after *x*'s conversion, can this equation be formulated in probabilistic terms. Only then has the intention become fully conscious. Hence, the initial probability equation allowing only for one state or the other would be absurd for an organism possessing any form of consciousness-memory. It could only pertain to an organism with very little to no memory that is limited to a one-dimensional either-or purpose.

In the situation just described any human act of conversion to a new perspective or belief can become the/a "real world." Afterward, an almost instantaneous consciousness of this "real world" can be generated, though in the beginning it was not so conscious. Our perspective of our/a "real world," then, whether scientific, artistic, or otherwise, is our *Total Consciousness.* In other words, *our consciousness is our "world," and the limits of one are the limits of the other.* This assertion is not meant to be merely a platitude, but the only possibility in light of the previous axioms, propositions, and inferential statements in this inquiry. The same idea has been articulated often by some of our most eminent scientists. For example, Schrödinger (1958, 52):

> The reason why our sentient, percipient and thinking ego is met nowhere within our scientific world picture can easily be indicated in seven words: because it is itself that world picture. It is identical with the whole and therefore cannot be contained in it as part of it.

5.112 What is the upshot of all this? First, our "real world" is by and large what our consciousness and our expectations of it dictate. Second, possessing memory, we are capable, by the fusion of space-time events within our "real world," of distinguishing ourselves here and now from that which existed there and then. Such a distinction implies the conception/perception of temporal *difference*, and such *difference* implies change, no matter how minute. Eventually and inexorably, as time-bound organisms we ourselves become a *difference*, a space *differentiated* from other spaces. We come to possess awareness of our self, which is at once inside itself and beside itself. This conscious self is destined to oscillate perpetually between existence within, as a self-contained space, and existence without, as a space contiguous with others and marked off by a sign. *We become a sign* (cf. Peirce, 1960, 5.313, according to whom man/mind is a sign).

Admittedly what I am describing is an extremely basic form of memory, consciousness, and temporality: a rather mythical account of their origin. Recall and perception of time are certainly for the human organism much more complex. Yet what can the atemporal present be but part of a process? What can time-awareness in the present be other than, as Whitehead tells us, fleeting memories of the past tinged with anticipations of the future? What is time that we, a vast collection of time-bound particle-waves, can be conscious of it, and what are we that we can possess consciousness of our conscious self through time?

I believe we must attempt to confront these questions in any viable inquiry into the *foundations* of written texts. Meanings in texts are conceived/perceived "in a flash," but texts can only be written/read over time. Two types of activity are involved here: a discovery and its proof, a creation and its elaboration, an intuition and its development. The first of these types of activity without consciousness is empty; consciousness without the second type of activity is barren.

Chapter 6
Parts and Wholes

6.10 Our Perception of the Written (and Spoken) Sign

6.11 Let us for the moment leave conceptual spaces and their materialization to discuss specifically how names (words) are represented as marks-on-paper in written texts (6.12-6.18). Then we will be in a position to understand how an organism's knowledge can become embedded (tacit consciousness) (6.21-6.33), and how the organism can acquire new knowledge (7.11-7.29). Within this framework I will postulate a model for the perception of written texts (7.31-7.35) and subsequently the embedment of knowledge in texts (7.41-7.48).

6.12 According to Vygotsky (1962, 126) when a child learns a language he:

> starts from one word, then connects two or three words; a little later, he advances from simple sentences to more complicated ones, and finally to coherent speech made up of series of such sentences; in other words, he proceeds from a part to the whole. In regard to meaning, on the other hand, the first word of the child is a whole sentence. Semantically, the child starts from the whole, from a meaningful complex, and only later begins to master the separate semantic units, the meanings of words, and to divide his formerly undifferentiated thought into those units. The external and the semantic aspects of speech develop in opposite directions—one from the particular to the whole, from word to sentence, and the other from the whole to the particular, from sentence to word.[1]

What is this "one word," this "holophrastic" sentence the child begins with? If a sign, following Peirce, is something that represents something to someone in a given respect or capacity, then what is this second "something"? Is it something rigid, determinate, static, and universal? Is the relation between the two "things" that of a "mental-thing" and an "object-thing" in the world? Or is it intrinsic, existing solely in the mind, with no necessary nor absolute correspondence with the world?

Consider that, with respect to any inquiry into human cognition, the initial and most important relation between a name and that to which it refers is intrinsic (between a name and its conceptual boundary) and that the relation between them is never static. This implies an ongoing process, a continual moving back and forth from name (image) to boundaried space (concept) and from boundaried space to name, and from that boundaried space to other boundaried spaces and from that name to other names. During this process the relation between name and boundaried space inevitably undergoes changes. These changes can exist irrespective of any reference to the physical world.

In this sense an internally related name (A) is made to stand for its internal representation, a conceptual space (B), by the addresser (C), and this representation is "mapped into" a similar internal representation possessed by the addressee (D). According to this formulation, the material manifestation of (A) can be an uttered sound or some marks-on-paper. Or, (B) can be a concept about some concrete entity in the physical world or about something abstract that can be given physical representation, and so it possesses external reference. This is exemplified by the continuous or "traveling wave" pattern of oscillations in Figure 12.

On the other hand, if (C) and (D) have no external manifestation in the physical world, either soliloquy or "inner speech" (Vygotsky, 1962) occurs, or there may be discussion about purely formal or imaginary entities. For example, "square circles" can possess neither form nor representation; yet they can be talked about though not imagined. And "unicorns" can be imagined, talked about, and represented as marks-on-paper, though they do not exist in the physical world. Lacking external reference, names and boundaried spaces referring to "inner speech" or to such purely formal or imaginary entities can be illustrated by Figure 16.

6.13 Observe some examples of how internal representations influence perception of external manifestations. Draw a cross on a piece of paper and show it to a devout Christian in a chapel listening to a moving sermon. Boldly and irreverently ask him what it is. Assuming that he answers your question instead of smiting you on the cheek or telling you to shut up and listen, he will most probably not say: "It's just two marks-on-paper." Nor: "It is a geometric figure consisting of two straight black lines on white paper, one line approximately six inches long and vertically positioned, the other approximately five inches and horizontally positioned, with the first bisecting the second and the second cutting across the first approximately two inches from the top." His response will undoubtedly have something to do with crosses in the sense of Christ, crucifixion, sacrifice, atonement, salvation, and so on. In other words, he attends to the meaning rather than to the material manifestation of the sign-symbol. Attention to the marks-on-paper would destroy its intrinsic meaning.

Now write CROSS on the reverse side of the paper, take it to another member of the congregation, and ask him what it is. The response will undoubtedly be: "Cross." You tell him: "No, what I meant was what is it really?" After a quizzical look he responds: "It's a word with four letters that spells 'cross'." There is always a tacit resistance against attending to the bare physical manifestations of the sign. That is, the sign tends to be "transparent."

6.14 If on perceiving written words we are ordinarily only peripherally aware of the words themselves and maintain focal awareness on the meaning that lies behind the words, do we really "look beyond" the words as when peering through a window? What is meant by the analogy of a window pane and the "transparency of language"? Does this transparency necessarily imply awareness of marks-as-meaning and nonawareness of marks-as-marks? Consider that you are in a movie theatre watching a gory battle scene. At the instant when a soldier is bayoneted a few large red spots appear on the screen in such a way that it seems that drops of blood have splattered on the camera lens. Your attention, as a consequence, is automatically directed toward the omniscient but invisible camera. But did you not know all along that it was there? Did not signs such as ticket stubs in one hand, popcorn in the other, the screen, seats, and decor surrounding you, the entranced eyes peering in the same direction, tell you that it was all shot from a camera? "Willing suspension of disbelief" had placed you "inside" the action of the movie, but tacit awareness of the medium of the message was always there as well. You had become emotionally involved in the fiction before you, but yet you realized that it was not really "real" (for further detail, see Merrell, 1980b).

6.15 Likewise, when reading a book you attend to the marks-as-meanings but are you not somehow peripherally and nonconsciously aware of the marks-as-marks? What would it mean to say that writing is "nothing more" than marks-as-marks that represent something else to someone in some respect or capacity?

CAT is the material and arbitrary representation of a conceptual boundaried space. When the written word appears in the context of a text it is ordinarily perceived in "analog" fashion: all at once and as a continuous entity. But the word is actually made up of discontinuous concatenated parts upon which specific attention usually does not rest; the word is ordinarily assimilated *in toto,* whether written or spoken. On the other hand, poetic language, by "laying bare the device" according to the Russian formalists, tends to "force" the reader to focus on the language's "transparency," on the parts making up spoken words or on parts of the marks-as-marks in order properly to perceive rhythm, rhyme, alliteration, euphony, etc. For instance, the onomatopoeic "meow" of the CAT possesses necessary sound qualities which can be exploited by poetic language, and hence repetition of sound patterns of the word on the phonological level demands attention to it as-marks, and even to parts of it, for proper comprehension of a given poem.

However, the fact is that poetic sound patterns belong more properly to spoken words than to written and visual marks. An onomatopoeic word can be adequately sensed through the auditory channel only, or through visual perception of the corresponding marks-on-paper while "imagining" the auditory component of the word. But can it be properly sensed solely through the visual channel? Take the word "meow." If these four letters are perceived exclusively as-marks, nowhere in them do we find "onomatopoeia." Furthermore, if "w" is repeated throughout the stanza of a poem we can have visual redundancy but there is no necessary correlate between this graphic form of redundancy and the auditory redundancy by means of phonologically identical patterns that produce poetic rhythm, rhyme, alliteration, or whatever. It must be admitted that the graphic aspect of the written word is not a subset of nor is it subordinate to the auditory aspect of the spoken word. *The written word is a complementary mode of semiotic representation.*

6.16 However, there is one important mechanism, mentioned above, which is shared by both speech and writing: tacit and conscious awareness of parts and wholes and the contradictory situation it entails.

Either to write or to speak implies the following tacit proposition: "These meaningless marks-on-paper (or sounds-in-the-air) have meaning."[2] If the proposition is indeed true it must equally apply to itself, but this is of course an infinite regress, and it is also contradictory. If the marks (or sounds) are meaningless they cannot have meaning and if they have meaning they cannot be meaningless. Naturally, it could be countered that, given the phenomena of "double articulation," meaningless "atoms" can be arbitrarily combined to form compounds that are endowed with meaning by the dictates of social convention.

However, what would happen if we all suddenly forgot that words are in the beginning arbitrary: that is, meaningless with respect to that which they represent? What happens to Pavlov's dog when it takes the bell for the smell (the signal for the index)? Or when the dog interprets the nip as a bite? Or when the schizophrenic confuses three black marks-on-paper with a pointed instrument which threatens to kill him? Or when primitive man believes that if his enemy knows his name he will have power over him? In each case a (somewhat) arbitrary sign generated by a coding device is shorn of its indirect figurative and symbolic power, and it is confused with either a sign that ordinarily denotes something else or with the real thing that is ordinarily the denotatum of the sign. One form of sign either replaces another form, or the sign is transferred from its position of contiguity with its boundaried space to occupy that boundaried space or to become the boundaried space; that is, the map is confused with the territory. In this sense, it is as if we were at the top of a skyscraper looking down from a floor-to-ceiling opening, and suddenly realized that there was no window pane in the opening. Our security would be lost, for there would no longer be any "transparency" between ourselves, our "inner" self, and the world "out there." There would be no necessary linkage, for the two would be one.

Hence, there must be some sort of awareness, through "transparency," that a word is a meaningless set of marks or sounds if not connected to any specific boundaried space. And this awareness must ordinarily be tacit. However, the problem is that just as it is impossible to be simultaneously "inside" a language and translate from that language to another, so it is impossible to focus simultaneously and directly on the word-as-meaning and on the word-as-marks. We can only do either one or the other. And since attention at a given moment rests necessarily on one, the only way the other can exist in consciousness, albeit peripherally, is by means of the oscillatory model described in 5.18-5.19. By this model our attention can remain "outside" while we are tacitly aware of what is "inside." The paradox of "outside" and "inside" is thus resolved because, like Zeno's paradox, we ordinarily do not perceive it as being a paradox at all.

6.17 Now, with respect to the purely visual aspect of written words, it bears reiterating that we do not "see" things-as-they-are but always from some definite perspective.

Consider these two graphic schemata:

CAT   CⱯT

The distinction between them is obvious. In the context of a sentence that is in the context of a text, nevertheless, CⱯT may easily be read as CAT without immediate awareness of the distinction. In other words, since the whole is ordinarily detected in its context as a whole undifferentiated into its constituent parts, when one or more of those parts are permuted the whole is ordinarily perceived as unchanged.[3] In this light, Bruner and Postman (1949) have conducted an interesting experiment with playing cards, most of them normal but some of them contradictory, i.e., black hearts or red spades. The contradictory cards are almost always identified without hesitation as normal. Expectations took precedence over empirical evidence.[4]

6.18 Some other examples of how the mind contributes to the form and content of visual percepts:

(1) Recall those puzzles sometimes accompanying cartoon sections in newspapers that are composed of two rough drawings between which there are a half-dozen or so minor distinctions. At first glance the drawings, perceived in holistic fashion, appear to be identical. Only by breaking them up ("digitalizing" them) and analyzing the parts is it generally possible to find those distinctions. Then an amazing thing happens. Since the distinct parts are now part of our holistic awareness we can hardly glance at the drawings without seeing one, two, or more of the distinctions! Preliminary perception of these

drawings is "instantaneous" and spatial; then as the drawings are analyzed, perception becomes linearly organized through time. Similarly, CⱯT and CAT are ordinarily perceived "synthetically," "instantaneously," and spatially in the context of the texts; in contrast, to focus on the parts of the words in order to establish likenesses and distinctions is to "analyze" them through time.

(2) Consider the following:

Book / book
le livre

We invariably "see" the first line as a set of almost-equivalent words and letters, and we might even "see" the same word as being merely repeated. It is only with additional effort that we attend to the "real" differences between the two words or "see" them as no more than a collection of distinct shapes. On the other hand, the second line to the perceiver knowing absolutely no French can be nothing more than a nonsensical collection of "letters." However, he is capable of attending to the letters-as-letters, hence they are not merely a nonsensical set of abstract marks. With respect to the third line, we have no difficulty "seeing" the "eyes"-as-letters in the context of a meaningful word. The mind leaps to this conclusion without hesitation, especially since the two icons-as-eyes complement the meaning of the word that lies behind the two abstract marks-as-letters (Rescher, 1973).

Hence given certain situations and contexts, we automatically perceive either letters-as-words (while awareness of the letters-as-letters is tacit), letters-as-letters (without consciousness of the words they represent), or icons-as-letters-as words (while being "simultaneously" aware of the icons-as-letters and the letters-as-words). In the sections that follow I suggest that such "seeing" can be the result of continual embedment in our consciousness.

6.20 Expanded Tacit Knowing[5]

6.21 In light of the above, if "seeing" is always from some definite perspective, and if we generally tend to "see" what we knew we would "see" and what we expected to "see," then it can in a certain way be said that "seeing" is a form of knowing, knowing is cognition, and recognition is knowing again. To know again is to reconstruct a boundaried space that was previously "seen" either in the world or in the mind. Upon such reconstruction, the boundaried space, although manifested by the same material properties of sounds-in-the-air or marks-on-paper, can appear to become *condensed*. That is, with successive reconstruction and with habituation, it comes to signify more and more and it implies greater and greater tacit awareness. Consequently, consciousness of the particulars within these *condensed* boundaried spaces tends to become less and less.[6]

Hence there seems to be some "stretching" somewhere. Conceptual boundaried spaces appear to be amorphous. They can be *condensed* into increasingly abstract forms, yet tacit and nonconscious awareness of these spaces is at the same time increased to include an increasingly greater number of clustered boundaried spaces (cf. 5.11-5.15).

6.22 Some "thought experiments" follow to illustrate a particular aspect of this phenomenon.

(1) Someone gives me a lump of white stuff and tells me to eat it. After doing so, I exclaim: "It tastes exactly like sugar." But instead of that expression I might have exclaimed more primitively: "Sugar!" Did the substance sugar come before my mind? Did I spontaneously and consciously construct a boundaried space only for sugar before being able to emit the evocation? Or, as Wittgenstein (1970, 114e-16e) tells us:

> Can I say that this taste brought the name "sugar" along with it in a peremptory fashion? Or the picture of a lump of sugar? Neither seems right. The demand for the concept 'sugar' is indeed peremptory, just as much so, indeed, as the demand for the concept 'red' when we use it to describe what we see.
>
> I remember that sugar tasted like this. The experience returns to consciousness. But, of course: how do I know that this was the earlier experience? Memory is no more use to me here. . . . I am only transcribing my memory, not describing it.

Would "I" convey any less information in this particular situation by exclaiming, "Sugar!" than by saying, "It tastes exactly like sugar"? Imagine another situation. At the breakfast table someone asks me: "What will you have?" I reply: "Sugar." Does sugar mean the same here as it did in the previous situation? Is it the representation of the same boundaried space? No. The sound waves in the air may be almost identical but the boundaried spaces behind them differ. To the addressee goes the responsibility of comprehending the boundaried space by means of the linguistic context and the situation since the material manifestation of the boundaried space is only a schematic representation of the thought that motivated it. Hence, what remains tacitly implied behind the addresser's materialization of his boundaried space must be tacitly inferred by the addressee.

(2) Now imagine a carpenter on a scaffold ten feet high shouting instructions to his apprentice: "Ten penny!" "Two by!" "Cut on mark." And so on. None of these instructions constitutes a grammatically correct sentence. The sentences are *condensed;* either the subject or the predicate is omitted. This "simplified syntax" greatly reduces the number of words necessary for comprehension on the part of the workers. It is a more efficient means of communication since, within the situation, similar *condensed* boundaried spaces possessed by addresser and addressee can be relatively directly "mapped" onto brief *condensed* phrases. What is not explicit in the phrases is implicit, part of the tacitly known "language-game" in which the two participants are engaged (Wittgenstein, 1953, 9e-10e).

(3) You are with a like-minded friend in an art gallery. On rounding a corner you spot a painting and spontaneously emit an energetic: "Wow!" Your friend turns to see it and remarks: "Right on!" Or something equally inarticulate. Obviously you have communicated something to each other. But what precisely is that something? What explicitly did you mean by "Wow"? What did your friend mean by the complementary remark? Or, should the two expressions even need explication? Your initial perception of the painting was instantaneous, holistic, and "analog." You attended not to the parts for you had no time for any such thing. Your *condensed,* tacit, nonconscious awareness encompassed all the parts into a whole percept that obviously pleased both you and your friend.

If asked to explain in detail your reaction you might begin with something like: "Well, that colored shape in the upper left-hand corner is symmetrical with the one in the lower right corner but contrasts strikingly with. . . ." Now you are forced to attend to the parts, "analytically" breaking them down, noticing their interrelation, comparing and contrasting them, and so on. This is of course a radically different but complementary activity.

(4) Wittgenstein (1970, 19e) tells us:

> Let us imagine someone doing work that involves comparison, trial, choice. Say he is constructing an appliance out of various bits of stuff

with a given set of tools. Every now and then there is the problem "Should I use *this* bit?"—The bit is rejected, another is tried. Bits are tentatively put together, then dismantled; he looks for one that fits etc., etc., I now imagine that this whole procedure is filmed. The worker perhaps also produces sound-effects like "hm" or "ha!" As it were sounds of hesitation, sudden finding, decision, satisfaction, dissatisfaction. But he does not utter a single word. Those sound-effects may be included in the film. I have the film shewn me, and now I invent a soliloquy for the worker, things that fit his manner of work, its rhythm, his play of expression, his gestures and spontaneous noises; they correspond to all this. So I sometimes make him say "No, that bit is too long, perhaps another'll fit better."—Or "What am I to do now?"— "Got it!"—Or "That's not bad" etc.

If the worker can talk—would it be a falsification of what actually goes on if he were to describe that precisely and were to say e.g. "Then I thought: no, that won't do, I must try it another way" and so on— although he had neither spoken during the work nor imagined these words?

I want to say: May he not later give his wordless thoughts in words? And in such a fashion that we, who might see the work in progress, could accept this account?—And all the more, if we had often watched the man working, not just once?

It is impossible to separate the thinking (or the conceptual boundaried spaces) of this person from his activity. His thinking is part of his activity just as external speech by means of explicitly formulated and grammatically correct sentences would be intimately connected to his internal boundaried spaces. This form of thinking, or this form of relating conceptual boundaried spaces, is similar to Vygotsky's "inner speech" and to the "holophrastic" sentence described above. Inner speech, like related clusters of *condensed* boundaried spaces, is not merely the interior aspect of external speech, nor is it simply a condensation of external speech. In external and grammatically correct speech, thought is embodied in words. Many of the words in grammatically correct ("digital") speech disappear as inner speech (or related clusters of boundaried spaces) combine to form "analog" wholes of meaning. In contrast, *condensed* "inner speech," like *condensed* boundaried spaces, is to a large extent thinking without words, thinking with pure meanings (pure spaces) whose embodiment in words can only come later. Hence, "inner speech," like *condensed* boundaried spaces within particular situations, is dynamic, pliable, a perpetually changing process. For this reason direct communication between minds is by and large impossible. It occurs only indirectly and with a greater or lesser degree of imprecision by "mapping" similar clusters of *condensed* spaces into grammatically correct utterances.

6.23 The above "thought experiments" attest to the fact that clusters of *condensed* internal spaces ordinarily do not enjoy a one-to-one correspondence with grammatically correct externalized speech. These spaces, like the *condensed* expressions described above, represent a "stretching," that is, an increase or expansion of implied or tacit meaning, which occurs with habitual use of language. Clusters of *condensed* boundaried spaces entail conceptual matter that can be explicitly describable only by means of larger and larger grammatically correct statements, or they can be only partly explicit since part of them remains at implicit and tacit levels.

In the following section I will discuss the formation of these tacit levels that govern internal *condensed* boundaried spaces.

6.30 Learning about Tacit Knowing

6.31 According to Piaget (1926), between the ages of one-and-a-half and two years the child's reasoning ability is described as "sensori-motor." He "acts out" rather than "thinks" in adult fashion and his speech consists in "telegraphic" essentials. Gradually, as the child's mental structures develop he acquires the capacity to perceive and conceive "correctly" spatial, temporal, and causal properties, and to generate syntactically correct sentences and logically cogent propositions and arguments. In short, he is reaching the adult level of thinking. But for the moment interest lies at the first level.

It might appear plausible that the child speaking in "telegraphic" essentials does not factor his thought through the mesh of syntactically correct or adult grammar. He is concerned with more basic linguistic relationships such as agent-action, agent-object, action-object, possessor-possessed, etc. The child strives for expression of these relationships, and in so doing constructs utterances devoid of certain parts of correct speech (see Bloom, 1970; Schlesinger, 1971).

However, it is more proper to conceive of the child's rudimentary speech as something like the reverse of *condensed* adult speech. In this sense, the child's speech is similar to the *condensed* boundaried spaces and their *condensed* linguistic representation as described above. A "telegraphic" set of words is in whole or in part explicitly incomprehensible outside the pragmatic situation and outside knowledge of a proper syntactic component that is capable of placing the words into a grammatically correct sequence (McNeill, 1966). Basically the same can be said of *condensed* boundaried spaces. This indicates that the child's "telegraphic" utterances or the adult's conceptual boundaried spaces cannot stand alone. Their very existence in human cultures implies some atemporal principle of organization which imposes on them a generalized pattern.

What is this atemporal principle? If, as has been implied, strings of boundaried spaces are "spatially" organized, it is necessary, in order to communicate in a human culture, to translate these strings of boundaried spaces into temporally and serially organized words; that is, into utterances or marks-on-paper (see Lashley, 1951, on the brain's penchant for seriality). But at the same time, these utterances or marks-on-paper, to be intelligible, must be organized by means of an atemporal structuring principle; a set of grammar rules. Whether these grammar rules are innate or not is not the question here. The important point is that their existence bears on the interaction and interdependency between boundaried spaces and language, between memory and language, and between expression and content. If the child begins at the bottom and works upward from broad conceptual spaces and their *condensed* expression and thought to greater and greater explicitness by means of grammatically correct sentences, so the adult, through habit, convention, and by following pathways of least resistance, *condenses* his expression and thought while the boundaried spaces they represent are also *condensed*, and tacit awareness of them is concomitantly amplified. What was tacit can become explicit and what was well formed can become *condensed*.

6.32 A crucial distinction must be established here, however, between rules and strategies. We would suppose that grammar rules (the structuring principle) are invariant, or almost so. But they allow for flexible strategies, partly determined by the contingencies of pragmatic situations, for a large number or even over time a potentially infinite number of possible responses. Strategies are formulated within contexts and situations, and they involve varying degrees of explicitness and implicitness on the one hand, and varying degrees of tacitness and consciousness on the other.

The bee dance, although manifesting key properties of human languages such as arbitrariness, specialization, displacement in time, interchangeability, and synthesis of parts to form a whole message (productivity) (Hockett, 1959), entails strategies that are few in number and relatively invariant. Also, bees build hives by use of a relatively simple and invariant set of rules and by means of relatively inflexible strategies. From the bees to the "talking apes" there is a remarkable progress in terms of increasingly sophisticated strategies, and finally, at the human level, where N-N relations of potentially infinite range are possible, strategies become complexified to the extent that the rules are in some cases hardly apparent.

Moreover, at the human level of N-N relations, relatively invariant and even possibly innate (grammar or any other) rules can be used to generate a potentially infinite range of culture-bound conventional "games" that themselves entail explicitly or implicitly formulated rules many of which allow for a large or potentially infinite number of possible strategies.

6.33 The potentially infinite number of strategies and of "games," language or whatever I am speaking of ultimately involves metalevels of communication. For instance, consider the chess game. Two master players follow the "rules of the game" and develop their strategies almost nonconsciously. The rules have become embedded in their thought processes and the strategies have become *condensed* such that the players hardly use inner thought-words or boundaried spaces, let alone external speech-words, on "mapping" them out. The actual moves of both players are guided by the situation, and choices are made from a number of possible moves. However, if they begin arguing about the rules, about why certain rules exist, or about changing a rule to improve the game, they are now metacommunicating. This metacommunication reveals, at a higher level of abstraction, the real freedom provided for by "games" and rules constructed at the culture-bound level of N-N relations.

Similarly, to generate grammatically correct statements is to connect internal (and usually to a greater or lesser degree, *condensed*) boundaried spaces to their exterior manifestations. This activity implies prior knowledge of grammar rules. In addition, a second activity, the generation of statements about statements, presupposes the ability ultimately to learn about and talk about culture-bound rules of thought and of language use; that is, to talk about *condensed* boundaried spaces, and perhaps even about certain innate capacities.

The next chapter deals appropriately with learning at increasingly complex levels. This is a necessary step since, as I shall argue in the following chapters, the ability to properly construct/perceive written texts presupposes the ability to think and talk about signs, statements, and texts, and, through memory and learning, to construct/perceive successively *condensed* boundaried spaces.

Chapter 7

Learning to Learn

7.10 Preliminaries

7.11 The question in this chapter is: How can the organism learn to know about systems of signs and how can it know how to learn about them?

7.12 There are three assumptions on which this chapter is based:

(a) Knowing, on conscious and nonconscious levels, is derived from one's repertoire of boundaried spaces.

(b) A given repertoire of boundaried spaces involves contexts and relations.

(c) Learning occurs through knowledge, on conscious and nonconscious levels, of contexts and relations.

The contexts and relations in assumptions (b) and (c) can be placed into the following categories:

(a) Simple relations between boundaried spaces and the context of addresser and addressee (i.e., 1-2 and 1-N relations that involve messages conveyed primarily by inherited traits between members of the same species [gulls, bees, primates, etc.] or between members of different species ["dead" opossums, "lame" birds, etc.]).

(b) Relations between two (or in some cases, more) possible boundaried spaces and the relations within the context of addresser and addressee (i.e., 2-1 relations that are either inherited or learned [a peanut shell or an x on a box to denote a peanut inside, Pavlov's dog], 2-2 relations that are most probably chiefly inherited [nip-bite phenomena, play among primates] or learned [porpoise-human

play], and 2-N relations that are learned [possibly the "talking apes"]).
(c) Relations between potentially large sets oɪ boundaried spaces
and the relations within the context of addresser and addressee
(i.e., N-N relations, which, as will be discussed below, are probably
generally accessible only to human beings but which have been
occasionally— though perhaps erroneously—observed in the "talking apes").

7.20 Learning: Animal and Human

7.21 Compare 1-1 relations to a one-dimensional line, which, even
along the Möbius strip, is continuous with no indication of "digitalization," discontinuity, or "catastrophe." 1-1 relations represent "zero
information," and they can lead to no more than "zero learning," like
the iron filings, where no information is sought and response to "information reccived" is invariant. No change of response pattern is
possible.

This situation is also like the relatively passive "player" of a von
Neumannian game that is no more than a mathematical fiction. The
player is programmed to compute the solution to whatever problem
the game can present according to a fixed set of possible strategies.
The "player" always responds appropriately and in a predetermined
but probabilistic way to the information given. Since the response is
based on probabilities it is possible for the "player" to make a decision
that is found to be incorrect when additional information becomes
available. But the "player" is incapable of learning from its mistakes.
In other words, the discovery of this mistake can presumably contribute nothing to future decisions.

7.22 Now consider the three modes of learning outlined below
(which are, with a few changes, derived from Bateson, 1972, 279–
308).

Learning I. Compare 1-2 and 1-N relations to the flat surface of the
Möbius strip, which can be conceived as a two-dimensional continuous topological space broken by a discontinuous "catastrophe." Information received at the 1-2 level can be met either with a positive or
negative response or by choice from two contradictory alternatives.
The response can be either the result of coded instructions in the
nervous system of the organism or the result of learning. If it is the
result of learning, temporality becomes a factor insofar as at time 1
the organism did not respond "properly" to a given stimulus but at

time 2 it did. In other words, if the organism has learned, then the context surrounding the situation at time 2 has been perceived differently from the context at time 1. This learning can become habitual, embedded, part of the organism's "knowledge." Hence with additional reinforcement through time it responds more rapidly and more efficiently. The organism can also come to respond similarly to slightly deviant contexts. If a dog sees its master approach with a bag marked "FIDO BRAND DOG MEAL," it may respond in basically the same way whether in the back yard, in the kitchen, or in the basement. On the other hand, if the context is radically altered it might not respond to this marker at all; for example, if a total stranger enters the house and picks up the bag he might be met with a menacing growl.

Learning II. Compare the "Klein bottle" to 2-2 and 2-N relations. The "Klein bottle" is, like a three-dimensional continuous topological space, broken by a discontinuous "catastrophe." Learning II involves a two-way choice from a set or sets (ordered pairs) of alternatives, and from within the system those alternatives can be interchangeable. Certain responses to 2-2 relations are most probably innate in the nervous system in the case of canine, primate, and other forms of play activity. The nip, for example, is part of the bite, and it triggers play response that is "as if" a fighting response. Interchangeability of these alternative responses, as discussed above, occurs repeatedly in this natural process. Porpoise-human play and chimp-human play is undoubtedly learned, although this activity entails a similar set of alternatives. 2-N relations, which are on the other hand learned by primates and man, entail responses from a much broader range of alternatives. 2-2 relations imply the context of possible 1-2 relations, and 2-N relations imply the context of possible 1-N relations.

The ambiguous "spot" on the adult herring gull that can denote two different spaces, is a subset of, on a higher logical level, the nip-bite message, which can denote two possible complementary spaces. The first consists in a sign that elicits one of a set of possible responses, the second consists in a set of signs eliciting one of a set of responses. This second message system entails a "digital switch" from one type of activity to another, a sort of "category switch" involving distinct logical levels.

Similarly, an invariant response to a range of possible messages is a subset of a pair of alternative responses to a range of possible messages. Thus learning II appropriately exists at a metalevel with respect to learning I. This metalevel enables us to explain the existence of N possible alternatives. It also explains why learning II can be called "learning to learn" or "transfer of learning"—which Bateson calls "deuterolearning."

A chimp can learn that plastic tokens of varying sizes and shapes are "signs" that stand for "something." It "knows" that they are arbitrary, that they can be combined in different ways to form different messages, and that when it does so it is properly reinforced. It might also "discover" that the tokens can be combined in novel ways. In essence it has learned to change what it learned in learning I. It now "knows" not merely that a particular token gives a particular response; it "knows" what the token is for, it possesses "knowledge" about the tokens even though in general it cannot (does not) "talk" about them. In this manner learning II involves change in the way messages conveyed by signs in contexts are perceived and change in the use of these signs.

Finally, with respect to human situations, learning II entails not only "learning to learn" at the rudimentary level just described. Human beings are capable of developing exceedingly complex conceptual frameworks (Rescher, 1973) and world views (Berger and Luckmann, 1966; Kuhn, 1970; Laszlo, 1972). With a (perhaps) partly innate, partly culture-bound, and partly idiosyncratic view of the world a human being approaches new situations, interprets them, and acts on them on the basis of his previously acquired knowledge of the world. If he can make his perceptual reality fit into his conceptual frameworks within his world view, his knowledge and beliefs are "reinforced." If not, he may simply reject those anomalous parts of his percepts, or, like the schizophrenic, he may reject them in their totality and "see" what he really wanted (or was compelled) to "see" in the first place. Such application of knowledge within conceptual frameworks to new situations is compatible with the current "paradigm" view of the sciences (Kuhn, 1970; Feyerabend, 1975; N. R. Hanson, 1958; Polanyi, 1958).

Learning III. The analog model for N-N relations is appropriately "unimaginable"; hence a four-dimensional visual model is not possible. In human societies learning II, with respect to its holistic *Weltanschauung* dimensions, evolves into self-confirmatory and self-reflexive cosmologies (Polanyi, 1958). However, the very fact that these radically diverse human societies can exist, or that by extension incommensurable scientific paradigms can account for the same set of data, or that human beings are capable of at least partially "learning" new cultures or of being "converted" to new religious or different scientific paradigms, implies the existence of some conceptual realm of a higher logical type than learning II. It also implies a radical reorganization of what a human being previously learned. In other words, learning III requires the existence of the "metaperspectival framework" described above.

7.23 To begin discussion of learning III, consider the Kuhnian hypothesis. From within the conceptual framework derived from a particular world view held by a given individual within a scientific community, anomalies appear for which there is apparently no solution. These "loopholes" are closed in the most expedient way possible from within the system, but soon others crop up, and later there occurs a proliferation of contradictions that provoke a "crisis situation." At some indeterminate point the "scales" fall off this individual's eyes, and through a "leap of faith" he is "converted," by an "irrational" and "illogical" act and from within the "metaperspectival framework," to a radically new perspective. From within this world it seems, at the outset, that all those aggravating anomalies vanish.

Somehow in the process of this "conversion" new and previously inconceivable alternatives become evident, like, at a rudimentary level, the realization that the Gestalt diagram is not just two opposed faces but also in reality a vase. However, the situation is certainly not so simple as that. "Seeing" either faces or vase can be a controlled act. In contrast, the Kuhnian "conversion" is indeterminate and uncontrollable. On perceiving alternatively figure for ground or ground for figure in the Gestalt diagram, one is able to change them at will, that is, if one lives in a world where there are humanoid faces and vases; in a world without vases the diagram might eternally depict two faces. Nevertheless, assuming that one can alter the two incompatible perspectives whenever one pleases, it follows that there must be some other level, a metalevel of higher logical type, from which the alternatives are generated. And, since indeterminate and uncontrollable Gestalt "switches" between broad perceptual frameworks obviously can occur, there must exist a corresponding metalevel that is potentially infinite in extension. This is, properly speaking, the "metaperspectival framework" (see Merrell, 1980b, 1980c, for further discussion).

7.24 Hence this metalevel entails various forms of activities. In its simpler forms it can be either controllable or uncontrollable, depending upon the consciousness of the perceiver. In its more complex forms it is chiefly uncontrollable.

Recall the alternating act of attending focally to the meaning lying behind the sign and peripherally to the sign itself (see 6.15). Reconsider being "inside" one language or alternately translating from that language into another (see 5.16). Or, on a more holistic and cosmological plane, recall the act of "conversion" from one religion to another radically distinct religion (see 3.31). All these phenomena are analogous to, at exceedingly more simple levels, puzzles, riddles, jokes, and puns.

7.25 Let us consider some examples of transitions to broader frameworks of higher logical type such that puzzles or riddles can be resolved, or analogously, such that jokes and puns can be understood.

(1) A puzzle:

• • •

• • •

• • •

Figure 17

The objective is to connect all dots, with four straight lines and without lifting the pencil from the paper. Ordinarily a person tries out all possible combinations while remaining inside the set of dots. Only by focusing attention outside the parameters of the nine dots is a solution possible, like this:

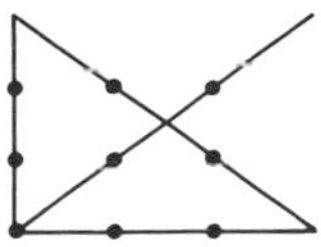

Figure 18

It was necessary to move outside the normal frame to "see" the situation from within the larger metalevel frame. That is, the system was opened and new rules and consequently new strategies were made possible (see Fry, 1963; Watzlawick, 1977; Watzlawick, Weakland and Fisch, 1974).

(2) A riddle:

"What is full of holes and holds water?"—a sponge.

The boundaried spaces and the list of names that usually come to mind is the "class of things that hold water." But the normal conception of this class of things pertains to objects without holes in them in the normal sense. Resolution of the riddle demands conception of some object outside the ordinary class of things within one's conceptual framework. In short, one must breach the boundaries of one's normal classification in order to perceive a new form of classification and hence solve the problem.

However, awareness of the contradiction does not necessarily accompany awareness of the solution. Consider this riddle:

> A car carrying a father and his young boy skids and plunges down a ravine, killing the father and placing the boy in critical condition. The boy is rushed to the hospital and the surgeon assigned to him exclaims, upon beginning examination, "I cannot operate on this patient. He is my son." How is the relationship of the surgeon to the boy explained?

Now, following our accustomed pathways of thought, this riddle presents a dilemma of which we are immediately aware. We think up a few weak and inadequate solutions involving illicit sexual relations, mistaken identity, and so on. But does it readily occur to us that the surgeon could be female, therefore the boy's mother? This association would ordinarily represent a (conscious or nonconscious) deviation from our normal channels of thought to conjecture a broad range of alternative possibilities: a broader system. This is an exceedingly difficult task at times. However, we all do it occasionally on nonconscious levels, such as when the answer to a problem suddenly occurs to us "in a flash." To learn to do it is to cultivate a capacity for deviating from normal thought channels.

7.26 The above examples illustrate that without breaching boundaries and opening systems from within broader perspectival frameworks, solutions to problems, puzzles, riddles, and so on are not forthcoming. Learning III requires the ability to bring about such transformations at increasingly more complex metalevels.

Learning III thus entails higher levels of awareness wherein the organism is able to open its customary systems and combine and recombine sets and classes of schemata and relations. Learning III must include, as subsets, learning I and learning II. It is a shift to a higher level of abstraction, from absolutes to the generation of alternative sets of schemata and interaction between schemata. Consequently, it entails alternative sets of rules for perceiving and conceiving the world. Learning III also affords greater ability to cope, over time, with changing situations. Hence, the empirical world can be more effectively ordered in different ways through the creation of new superordinate rules.

Learning I, II, and III do not correspond directly to levels of "intelligence," at least insofar as it is "measured" in our society. An ape can learn to do menial operations more effectively than a child. A computer can be programmed to play a better game of chess than most adult human beings. If "intelligence" is determined by the amount of new information that can be assimilated and the number of problems that can be solved by use of an invariant set of rules within a closed system, then humans have little to no advantage over the higher animals and machines. The vexing syndrome we confront is that success in our modern society is most rapidly achieved by following fixed procedures; we learn that it is wise not to look beyond the barriers of our closed systems lest we and our "superiors" become aware of our "ignorance." That is, use of learning III, which entails creativity in general, is discouraged, if not repressed.

7.27 In each of the above cases, while conscious and focal awareness might rest exclusively "inside" one framework, tacit awareness can exist "outside" it or in some other metaframework. The fact that in certain cases we can bring about a "switch" in our perceptive mode from one system to another at will implies that somehow there is some other system, a higher system, that is capable of encompassing both perspectival modes "simultaneously." Does such a metasystem (at broader levels, the "metaperspectival framework") have a bearing on what we conceive and perceive to be "real" and what we conceive and perceive to be "irreal"? Let us see, with respect to the production and reception of written texts.

7.30 How Texts are Perceived

7.31 Tentatively define all texts as series of signs (marks on paper) and their attendant boundaried spaces. When we read texts we may perceive them to be "true" with respect to what we ordinarily conceive/perceive to be the "real world" (i.e., in the Kuhnian sense, a scientific or religious text written from within a paradigm shared by the reader). At the other extreme, we may look upon them as being potentially or categorically "false" (i.e., for the scientist or religious person outside the paradigm from within which the text was written). In the case of artistic texts, folktales, myths, etc. they may be construed "as if true" or merely as "fictitious," or they may be viewed uncritically as "true." We necessarily bring expectations to all texts, and how we perceive them largely depends upon the nature of these expectations (Culler, 1975).

7.32 Now, consider reader response to literary texts in light of a variation of Coleridge's "willing suspension of disbelief." This phenomenon presupposes that we the readers first be somehow aware of our disbelief before we can willingly suspend it. Then we perceive the text on its own grounds while supposedly isolating the fictitious textual "world" from the "outside real world." If we suspend disbelief in this manner, we perceive in the text an imaginary world "as if" it really existed. In a sense it exists because we conceive it as constituting part of a "possible world."

For instance, as was tentatively suggested in 2.13, to talk about, say, a "square circle" "as if" it were "real" implies by the mere fact that we are using the words that a "square circle" has a certain kind of "reality." It is, or can be, "real" in a "possible fictitious world." However, when talking about a "square circle," we can say that it has no referent either in the objective material world or in the imaginary world of "logical" formulations, but that it can only be "as if real" in the purely fictitious world. In fact, it cannot even be "pictured" in the mind, only "said." Therefore, we exclaim with triumph that "square circles" are not really "real," that they cannot really exist.

But on so speaking we must have previously unsuspended our suspension of disbelief with respect not only to "square circles" but, by the same assertion, to all artistic (i.e., "nonreal") constructs. As such we are no longer participants in a given fictitious or "possible" (or "impossible" in a logical sense) world, but we are now spectators of that world with respect to our "real world." "Inside" a fictitious system, with disbelief suspended, all objects can be "real." On the other hand, "outside" the system, nonreference of objects, acts, and events from "within" the system can be conceived and so stated, but suspension of disbelief must have vanished. We can either suspend disbelief and all the terms in the system become self-referential and "real," or we can perceive nonreferentiality, and therefore "irreality" in the terms of the system, but *we cannot do both simultaneously.*

Consider, for example, an audience watching a 3-D movie. As they stare at the screen through their colored glasses, suppose a train appears to come right out of the screen and at them. Some of the spectators shrink back in fear. Why? Obviously, before the train scene, they watched the movie at a conscious level as a fiction; that is, as "real" from "within," since they had suspended disbelief in it. Yet obviously at a tacit level they were aware of the fiction-as-fiction, knowing full well that nothing projected on the screen could really harm them. Hence the fiction frame existed within the larger, but at this moment tacitly presupposed, "real world" frame. However, at the instant they reacted in fear of the approaching train, it was as if the fiction frame had become copresent, at the same level, with the "real world" frame. That is, nonconsciously, we must suppose, the fiction became for them really "real." Their response was unwilling, since nonconscious, and, after having become conscious of it, they could regain their composure, view the fiction-as-fiction once again, giggle nervously at their silly behavior, or whatever. But it was, according to the hypothesis presented here, impossible for them to be conscious of the fiction-as-fiction and the fiction-as-"real," within two distinct frames and at two levels, in *exact simultaneity.* (The "oscillatory model" adequately accounts for this *nonsimultaneity.*)

7.33 In the above sense the process of reading a literary text also involves paradox (see Merrell, 1978b, 1980c, 1980d, 1981a; and especially 1980b, for further work on fictions.). It is tantamount to accepting, with respect to the textual boundaries, this statement:

```
┌──────────────────┐
│ EVERYTHING WITHIN │
│    THIS FRAME     │
│       IS A        │
│     FICTION       │
└──────────────────┘
```

Figure 19

If the statement is itself a fiction it is true and hence it is not a fiction. If it is itself a true statement it is not a fiction and hence it is false. But if the statement is a fiction if, and only if, it is not a fiction, then somehow it must be "simultaneously" believed and not believed. But this is a contradiction, so how can we explain it? In our physical world what we accept as "real" we are compelled to believe and what is not "real" we ordinarily do not believe. On the other hand, concerning the world we put ourselves in when perceiving the literary text, our conscious disbelief and our willing suspension of disbelief must oscillate between "inside" and "outside." In other words, to suspend disbelief we must enter the text system (i.e., the fiction frame) and become a part of it. Yet the suspension is voluntary, and we must be at another level, but at the same time, "outside." This activity, to repeat, fits the oscillatory model described above.

7.34 Texts read from within scientific or religious paradigms (in the Kuhnian sense) follow similar lines of development. But there is an inversion here, for from within these cosmologies we must *involuntarily suspend disbelief*. That is, from within a scientific cosmology our notion of what to believe and what not to believe has become predetermined. Our expectations concerning what we will "see" are now embedded, and these expectations chiefly govern what texts we will perceive as "nonsense," "meaningless," or "false." Hence, when reading a text expected to be "true" or largely "true," our security in the particular cosmology it portrays will continue as long as we can cram our expectations into a Procrustean bed that consists of boundaries we have automatically assumed to be "real." We ordinarily do not conceive of these boundaries to have been conscientiously and intentionally drawn in the beginning by some predecessor (i.e., a shaman, mother or father, king, priest, scientist, college professor, god, etc.) through some concomitant *willing suspension of ontological disbelief*. Therefore, since we did not originally "think" these boundaries we are generally incapable of "thinking" beyond them, and we cannot ordinarily "see" and "say" what lies beyond. This is how the Newtonian-Cartesian paradigm, in its inception an "as if" hypostat, became dogma, blindly accepted on faith as a grandiose set of true propositions concerning the universe.

Consequently, the involuntary suspension of disbelief found in religion, ritual, myth, scientific paradigms, etc., allows things to be taken seriously that in another context would likely be dismissed—we no longer believe in phlogiston, certain "primitives" have difficulty believing in an intangible god, we do not believe that lightning represents the wrath of the gods, and so on. Involuntary suspension of disbelief from within a given cosmology can therefore be part of our culturally embedded knowledge. (Similarly, the nip might be construed as denoting the message "This fight is not a fight," synonymous with "This is play." This explains the rudiments of the same paradox at the level of animal play activity.)

It is important to note that contradiction inevitably lies behind our perceiving fictions. Nevertheless we are ordinarily aware of no contradictory situation: It is resolved nonconsciously, on a tacit level. This is because, while attending to the fiction "inside" the fiction frame, our awareness of what lies "outside" is tacit, and vice versa. Compare this situation to the riddles and puzzles illustrated above. When consciousness rests strictly "within" the riddle-without-the-answer, that answer, from "within" a broader frame, cannot be forthcoming. Similarly, when awareness rests exclusively "within" a fictional world, the "real world" cannot exist. Only by leaping "digitally" to a larger frame can one become aware of the answer to the riddle or the puzzle, or can one become aware of the "real world" against which the fictional world was constructed (see Merrell, 1980b, for further discussion).

7.40 What Is "Real"?

7.41 In this section we will see how, by returning to the primitive level of boundaried spaces, learning, belief, and "fictional" or "real" conceptual frameworks can become *embedded* in consciousness over time.

Boundaried spaces and their names are in the beginning directly, intrinsically, and presumably inseparably linked to conceptual boundaried spaces and their names. Hence the schemata (see also Merrell, 1980c):

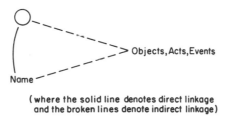

(where the solid line denotes direct linkage
and the broken lines denote indirect linkage)

Figure 20

By means of this intrinsic model of signs, names can come to represent *embedded* boundaried spaces that might otherwise be represented by other names under other conditions. That is to say, spaces are dynamic, they constantly *condense* or *decondense*. Names, on the other hand, remain relatively static. Let us now, by means of AXIOMS I-IV, demonstrate this phenomenon.

7.42 Mark off a boundaried space, and then mark off the same space again: $\bigcirc\bigcirc$. The two spaces must be marked off in succession. According to the oscillatory model described in Chapter 5, both spaces cannot be marked off at precisely the same instant: *There are no simultaneities.* Now *embed* the first space within the second: $\textcircled{\bigcirc}^1$. This *embedment* must occur during yet another increment of time; but, of course, in real-life situations such *embedment* ordinarily occurs nonconsciously.

Notice that $\textcircled{\bigcirc}$ is the same as if it were the second space. That is: $\textcircled{\bigcirc} = \bigcirc$. Hence, one space *embedded* within what is conceived to be an identical space is the same as the result of AXIOM I. In other words:

$$(\bigcirc\bigcirc = \bigcirc) = (\textcircled{\bigcirc} = \bigcirc).$$

Notice also that this is the same as the first *contraction* operation from 5.12. Thus:

$$(\bigcirc\bigcirc \rightarrow \bigcirc) = (\textcircled{\bigcirc} \rightarrow \bigcirc).$$

The problem is that for the ideal self-aware organism, $\bigcirc$ cannot be "absolutely identical" to $\bigcirc$ since there is a degree of change, no matter how small, from one "oscillation" "inside" and "outside" to another "oscillation." However, since the real organism possesses only a finite and discontinuous memory, the possibility of its absolutely complete and consistent recall of a relatively complex space from one "oscillation" to another is virtually impossible. Consequently, it "images" identity and continuity where none actually exists. It "images" identity like it "images" continuity when viewing a movie consisting of a certain number of discontinuous and static frames flashing on and off per second, or analogously, like it "images" continuity in overcoming Zeno's paradox.

In addition, notice that if $\textcircled{\bigcirc} = \bigcirc$, it is the same as if the first space had been crossed and then recrossed. That is: $\textcircled{\varnothing} = \bigcirc$. The overall result is the same as if we applied AXIOM II. It is also the same as the second *contraction* operation. Hence:

$$(\varnothing \rightarrow \text{\textemdash}) = ([\textcircled{\varnothing} \rightarrow \bigcirc] - [\bigcirc \rightarrow \bigcirc])$$

Now, give the first space a name. Call it x: $\bigcirc\!\!\smile x$. Call the second space x also: $\bigcirc\!\!\smile x$. As a consequence of the above, you can have:

$$\bigcirc\!\!\smile \underline{x} \;+\; \bigcirc\!\!\smile \underline{x} \;=\; \left(\bigcirc\!\!\smile \underline{x}\right)\!\smile \underline{x}$$

Differentiate the first calling from the second through an "oscillatory" increment of time by subscripts 1 and 2. Now you have:

$$\left(\bigcirc\!\!\smile \underline{x}_1\right)\!\smile x_2$$

Notice that according to Axiom III (that is, if we disregard the self-aware organism's memory), $x_1 x_2 = x_2$. It follows then that:

$$\left(\bigcirc\!\!\smile \underline{x}_1\right)\!\smile \underline{x}_2 \;=\; \textcircled{\bigcirc}\!\smile \underline{x}_2$$

Notice also that this is the same as if x_1 were negated according to Axiom IV. That is: $x_1 + \text{not } x_1 = \underline{\quad}$. Hence:

$$\left(\bigcirc\!\!\smile \underline{x}_1\right)\!\smile \underline{x}_2 \;=\; \textcircled{\bigcirc}\!\smile \underline{x}_2 \;=\; \bigcirc\!\!\smile \underline{x}_2 .$$

C**OROLLARY** IV: *Embedment of spaces and names into consciousness is the same as crossing and then recrossing spaces, and naming and then negating names.*[2]

7.43 Some examples of the above operations are in order.

(1) According to the initial preliminaries (cf. 1.12 and 1.13), boundaried spaces precede their names, therefore in the beginning they are not yet linked. And, according to the assertions in 6.10, internal and *condensed* boundaried spaces need not necessarily enjoy a one-to-one correspondence with the words in grammatically correct linguistic formulations that represent these spaces.

Hence, let μ denote the absence of a name (the empty name) that exists in the beginning; only a nameless boundaried space exists. Let that boundaried space be "horse + horn." The boundaried space is at this point connected to μ. Let the name attached to the boundaried space be "unicorn" (U). We now have A.

$$(A)\quad \left(\!\left(\underset{\text{I}}{\bigcirc}\right)\!\smile\mu \underset{\text{II}}{\smile}\right)\!\smile U$$

where space I represents "horse + horn" and space II represents "unicorn." Space I is "synonymous" with space II but the two are separated in time, due to the "oscillatory model" of conception/perception. Therefore they actually differ, even though only slightly, with respect to the context. The unnamed space existed within context I at time 1, and its naming occurred within context II, which must be different since the name was previously absent, at time 2.[3]

(2) A similar operation applies to a "dead" metaphor. Let μ denote the architectural style during a time in history that later came to be known as the "baroque" period. Let "baroque$_1$" (B_1) be the Portuguese word for "irregular pearl" (which was the original nonmetaphorical meaning of the word). Let "baroque$_2$" (B_2) denote a certain period in history (for which the term "baroque" is a metaphor; but the original meaning of the term has been lost, and hence it is ordinarily used literally to denote that particular historical period). Hence B.[4]

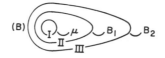

(3) Now, with a quantum leap, consider a unified and deeply *embedded* boundaried space depicting an entire world view, say, the Cartesian "machine model" of the universe. Let μ denote a unique and complexly abstract conceptual space that is correlated with the universe. Let U_1 denote the universe conceived as being "like" a "machine," and let U_2 denote the whole universe conceived to be literally a machine (that is, when the metaphorical quality of this Cartesian-Newtonian scientific model has become embedded). And finally, let U_3 denote the concept of the parts of the universe (i.e., atoms, lower organisms, human beings, planets, etc.) as machines in their structure and function (due to further embedment). Hence C.[5]

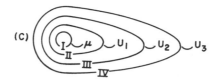

(4) Primitive "word magic" is also describable by these same operations. Let μ denote an emotionally charged conceptual space, say,

"communism = evil." Let HS denote the emblem of the "hammer and sickle" on the Russian flag, which is perceived not merely as a symbol of Russia, communism, the Kremlin, or some such thing, but *is literally evil* for a particular phobic anticommunist. That is, the symbol has become for him "as if" the "real thing," just as the map is sometimes confused with the territory, the forest with the trees, or the signal with the index. Hence D.

where the "word" remains inside the boundaried space and where indirect linkage between space, word, and sign becomes, for the conceiver/perceiver, direct. That is:

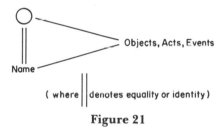

Figure 21

Such "word magic" is common. In the *Book of John* the word becomes God. Similarly, the name of god in many religions throughout time and space is conceived to be sacred. It possesses supernatural powers and is hence unutterable, for it *is* God. Personal names as well are in primitive societies believed to be not mere symbols, but part of the personal property of their bearer so that what is done to the name affects the person in the same way (Cassirer, 1946). Such belief in the magical power of words exists to a greater or lesser degree in all cultures and takes the form of superstitions, curses, witchcraft, taboos, and forms of wishful thinking. A common modern example of the belief in "word magic" is the hesitancy to speak of possible dangers. In an airplane to speak of a crash might be looked upon as somehow potentially causing it to crash (Ogden and Richards, 1923). Moreover, at the roots of "primitive" magic is the assumption that words precede their object of reference, that the word is intrinsic in the properties of the object. A study of children's thought reveals a similar phenomenon. For instance, ask a child why grass is grass and he might respond: "Because it is green." Or, ask him why ice is cold, and he might reply: "Because it is not hot" (see Piaget, 1969).

7.44 In all of the above examples spaces and names have become *embedded*, through habitual use or perhaps even some form of "repression," such that the sign user is ordinarily no longer consciously aware of at least some of the reasons for which he uses his signs, and identities are imagined where they otherwise would not exist, or where they otherwise would exist as *differences*. The *embedded* spaces and names can be either part of his tacit awareness—in which case by willfully altering his focus of attention he can become conscious of them—or they can exist in the nonconscious—in which case they are, with some degree of difficulty, retrievable, or they are wellnigh impossible to retrieve. *Embedment* understandably can be public (the Cartesian model, "communism," the baroque period, etc.) entailing a broad spectrum from world views and cosmologies to culturebound ideologies and prejudices to "dead" metaphors. Or, *embedment* can be private and idiosyncratic, the extreme case being that of the schizophrenic who actually "sees" unicorns.

7.45 Operations A, B, C, D, described by the above *embedments*, demonstrate that the various levels of consciousness can be effaced, like uncannily extracting the layers of an onion from its core outward:[6]

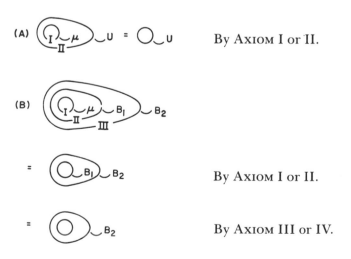

(A)　　　　　　　　　　　　　By AXIOM I or II.

(B)

　　　　　　　　　　　　　　By AXIOM I or II.

　　　　　　　　　　　　　　By AXIOM III or IV.

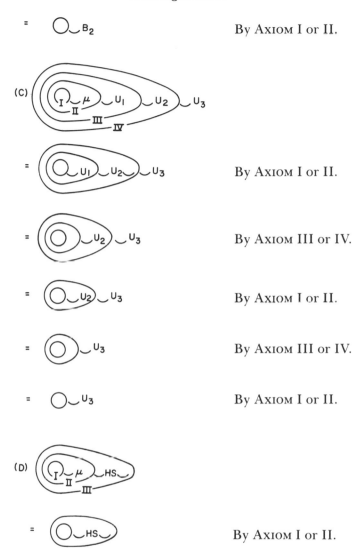

= $\bigcirc$ B_2 By Axiom I or II.

(C)

=   By Axiom I or II.

=   By Axiom III or IV.

=   By Axiom I or II.

=   By Axiom III or IV.

= $\bigcirc$ U_3 By Axiom I or II.

(D)

=   By Axiom I or II.

= $\bigcirc$ = $\bigcirc$ By Axiom I or II, and by negation of the name (Axiom IV).

7.46 Scientific world views and models, religious cosmologies, myths, ideologies, dogma, superstition, individual belief, even down to simple metaphors and puns, can, although at times erroneously, by an

increasing number of boundaried spaces be reduced to simple propositions (i.e., "God is love," "The universe is a machine," "The earth is
the center of the universe," "Man is inherently good, . . . or evil," "All
men are created equal," and so on). Conversely, by tracing the steps
upward by means of which these propositions were constructed, and
by reconstructing all the boundaries, the most elaborate world view
can be revealed from the simplest of propositions.[7]

Hence:

PROPOSITION V: *Human communicative systems are characterized by increasingly deeper degrees of embedment and by increasingly higher metalevels.*

7.47 What is needed, in order to retrace the steps of *embedment* and
to move into higher metalevels, is awareness of category mistakes,
contradictions, and paradoxes in conceptual systems. Such awareness
presupposes the ability to communicate about category mistakes, contradictions, and paradoxes from within increasingly larger systems. It
also presupposes awareness of vagueness, ambiguity, and overlapping
conceptual zones in human systems of classification.

Classification, one type of abstraction accessible in rudimentary forms
to all organisms, is an either-or affair. A class of things is determined
by some idea or concept that represents its defining characteristic
such that all items of experience must fall either "inside" or "outside"
it; they must fit into ready-made slots. A much more sophisticated
form of abstraction is the *comparative mode,* which includes classification as a subset and which is the basis for metaphorization and metonymization. The comparative mode is determined by relations and
network sets of relations, and by contexts rather than by classes. "Hot"
and "cold" are classes, but "hotter" and "colder," "warmer" and "cooler,"
require comparisons between items of experience in terms of the
logical relations of symmetry, transitivity, and reflexivity (see Carnap,
1966; Hempel, 1965). Furthermore, "blue-sound," "high-minded,"
"policemen-pigs," "man-lion," or "car-wheels" equally require such
comparison between items of experience in terms of metaphor and
metonymy.

Awareness of vagueness, ambiguity, and overlapping zones, in addition, entails the possibility of doubt, uncertainty, disbelief, skepticism, and cynicism. These states of mind presuppose that belief,

certainty, faith, and commitment are possible. If, as was described above, learning II becomes habitual through repetition, then it is possible for a human being to construct a general picture of the world that he believes is the correct one and that predisposes him to perceive objects, acts, and events in a particular way and to act on the world along partly predetermined paths. It also presupposes that another picture of the world can be forthcoming only by the aforementioned "leap of faith" and "conversion" from within the domain of learning III: the "metaperspectival framework."

In the next chapter I begin to tie in the hypothesis of learning III presented above with the notion of communication about category mistakes, contradictions, and paradoxes (that is, problem situations) as they are perceived in written texts.

Chapter 8
Aspects of a Viable Theory of Texts

8.10 I will assume that we agree on the following:

(a) Unlike lower animals genetically organized to respond to their environments in relatively fixed and determinate ways, humans must in addition, consciously as well as nonconsciously, organize themselves on social and personal levels. During the process of socialization they internalize a culture, a language, and a world view.

(b) The possession of a human culture, a human language, and a holistic world view, all of which can be spoken about at ever-increasing metalevels, distinguishes the human species from all other species.

The question is: How does this internalization (learning process or indoctrination) occur, and what makes it uniquely human? A preliminary answer to this question is necessary in order to understand how socially acceptable written texts are constructed. Once again let us begin with a conjecture and build up.

8.20 Two Assumptions

8.21 (1) *All organisms have a "philosophy" whether they realize it or not.*

It would be a misnomer to call this philosophy merely "instinctive behavior," "intuition," or "feelings." More appropriately stated, this philosophy is defined by a set of "expectations" possessed by an organism concerning the nature of a particular context or of all possible contexts (Popper, 1972). Many expectations, especially in the lower organisms, are inborn. The nestling herring gull is genetically conditioned to "expect" a red spot on the bill of adult members of the species, and it "expects" food when it pecks at that spot. The frog inherently "expects" that small dark spots that move in its field of vision are "bugs." Even the flatworm to a degree queries its environment in a trial-and-error way. It seeks information from its environment, and when it receives the information it "expects," it wants success (Count, 1969). That is, the flatworm, like all lower organisms, does not like to make mistakes. In this respect, a principal difference between the flatworm or the "amoeba and Einstein is that, although both make use of the method of trial and error elimination, the amoeba dislikes to err while Einstein is intrigued by it: he consciously searches for his errors in the hope of learning by their discovery and elimination" (Popper, 1972, 70).

The (conscious and nonconscious) philosophy possessed by all organisms is like a *hypothesis* that determines expectations that can be satisfied by trial-and-error elimination of items of experience in the environment. While certain expectations are innate, others can be learned by this successive trial-and-error process, and as a consequence certain expectations can be altered somewhat so that the organism becomes more adequately adapted to its environment or to new environments. The trial-and-error I speak of is not blind. It is nonrandom and selective since the expecting organism already "knows" what it wants from its environment and chooses only those items of experience that might possibly satisfy those expectations.[1]

8.22 (II) *All (conscious or nonconscious) philosophies presuppose the search (desire, need) for an orderly universe.*

The lower organisms, abhorring mistakes, are therefore "dogmatists." They possess "totalitarian mentalities." Creatures of instinct and habit, they approach and act upon new problem situations in fundamentally the same way. Comparatively few degrees of freedom exist for them, they usually enjoy few to no alternatives, and they respond to stimuli in terms of either-or categories. Nevertheless, conflict is at the same time for them minimized. Since stimuli are put into a category or they are categorically excluded from consideration, there is little or no vagueness, ambiguity, or uncertainty. There hardly exists any conceptual apparatus with which to generate alternatives. The result is closure of all items of experience into the same static system of responses by means of a relatively invariant set of rules. Hence when conflicting or "double-bind" situations are placed before an animal, like the dog that can no longer distinguish between the circle and the oval that are made to approximate one another in shape, it manifests signs of "neurosis."

Human beings also tend toward dogmatism and totalitarian minds. This is understandably the pathway of least resistance, where all is crystal clear, and where there are no unresolved problems. It is also indicative of a need all human beings have for regularity, "the need which makes them seek regularities; which makes them sometimes experience regularities even where there are none; which makes them unhappy and may drive them to despair and to the verge of madness if certain assumed regularities break down" (Popper, 1972, 23-24). True, when one is at a loss of problems everything appears simple; one's insecurity at least temporarily appears to have vanished. But, in truth, prolonged loss of problems would over the long haul spell death to all creative human efforts (Wittgenstein, 1970, 82ff). Tension, problems, uncertainty, vagueness, ambiguity, contradiction, and paradox are ultimately necessary, for without them ever-increasing metalevels of thought and language would be severely limited.

How, then, is this totalitarian mentality to be avoided? According to Popper, by the active and conscious search for problem situations that place acquired hypotheses in jeopardy, by criticism of the errors in those hypotheses, by maintenance of an open attitude of criticism such that all hypotheses and expectations are constantly improved and perpetually new problem situations are always met with new alternatives. Uncertainty, vagueness, ambiguity, contradiction, and paradox must be welcomed as a challenge to the mental capacity of the organism for generating newer sets of alternatives. Popper's (1972, 71) fundamental theorem follows:

> All acquired knowledge, all learning, consists in the modification (possibly the rejection) of some form of knowledge, or disposition, which was there previously, and in the last instance of inborn dispositions.

Significantly, what I have described in the preceding paragraphs terminates in a uniquely human situation. That is to say, all human learning consists of "the modification (possibly the rejection) of some form of knowledge" possessed previously. Such modification entails *changes in modes of thinking and subsequently in modes of action.*

8.30 Learning and Modes of Action

8.31 Let us begin with learning I and once again work upward. Learning I imprints an irreversible mode of action that is subject to little or no correction or revision: It is "dogmatic." It entails relatively fixed responses to a given set of situations: 1-2, 2-1, and 2-2 relations. There are no or few alternatives, there exists little or no freedom. Consequently behavior is determined by external objects, acts, and events. The mode of action resulting from learning I is one-dimensional and vertical: from a situation downward to a fixed mode of action.

8.32 With respect to the animal world, learning II entails more abstract modes of action. It also entails an increasing degree of freedom. Alternatives can be generated although they are few in number, usually only two. However, two alternatives lead to the possibility of an ambiguous situation and therefore conflicts can arise. But at the level of learning II there is little or no awareness of the conflict, for rules of action derived from learning II are fixed by external determinants. The organism cannot communicate or think about those rules, and consequently it is incapable of changing them.

Learning II, with respect to the human organism, reveals the possibility of a dramatic increase of alternatives over time with a concomitant decrease in dogmatism and absolutism. This process is similar to that described by Peirce's (1960, 5.388-5.410) four steps that lead to action. We begin with sensations of which we are immediately conscious. Successions of sensations lead to associations between sensations, and then a thought is created. The goal of thought is eventually the belief (or in Popper's terms, hypothesis or expectations) that certain things are the case under certain conditions. And this belief predisposes us toward a particular mode of action (or embedded belief) in particular situations.[2]

Now, the expansion of belief to include an increasing variety of percepts, concepts, and modes of action entails the gradual acquisition of a general world view concerning "the way things are." Actions from within this world view tend to follow social conventions, to become habits of thought and perception, to become a set of pathways of least resistance. In other words, percepts, concepts, and actions can become *embedded* such that, like playing a piano, driving a car, walking, etc., we simply do it without specific consciousness of what we do or how we do it. These *embedded* modes I speak of are part of our tacit awareness; they are part of the way we believe the world to be. At the same time, while awareness of the whole (i.e., general belief and world view) diminishes, there can be an accompanying increase of awareness concerning specific problem situations at the level of the sub-wholes. As we become increasingly conscious of our activity at this subwhole level minor conflicts are neatly dispensed with; we can become more critical, more demanding. But in so doing, awareness at the level of the whole tends to become less and less.

An example. The more we ride a bicycle the less aware we need to be of our activity as a whole. It becomes part of our tacit awareness. We can subsequently focus attention more effectively on the sub-wholes in order to improve our skill, say, in preparation for a race: leg rhythm, maximum use of a variety of muscles, body position, gear-shifting at the proper moment, turning angle on the curves, breathing, "rest periods," etc. Concomitantly, awareness of the bike-riding activity as a whole (i.e., maintaining ourselves in an upright position) becomes more and more *embedded*. With respect to this activity we simply let our body take care of itself. We just do it "without thinking."

Since this tacitly *embedded* knowledge that is derived from learning II is not knowledge about rules and possible changes of rules, it is necessarily two-dimensional: vertical arrangement, which entails a set of possible actions as a response to a given set of situations, but also horizontal arrangement between those situations and those actions. However, among the lower organisms this horizontal arrangement rarely exceeds two entities of choice. For instance, with respect to innate responses, the guard bee can receive either the community scent or a foreign counterscent to which it can manifest either "friendly" or "bellicose" behavior, but these responses are rigidly programmed. A dog can receive either a whole message (the bite) or part of that message (the nip) to which it can respond with play activity or war activity. Here there can be ambiguity and misunderstanding; it is not simply an either-or situation but a more-or-less situation, given the metonymical nature of the message. Learned responses outside the higher primates are usually limited to a similar scheme: a dualistic discontinuous or ambiguous and continuous situation.

8.33 Learning III. Imagine two people playing checkers who are unable to speak each other's language. Each begins by rigidly following fixed rules while developing a strategy for defeating his opponent. At one point in the game one player moves a checker piece outside the board to an imaginary square in order not to be "jumped." This gesture exists at the metalevel. It indirectly brings into question one or more of the rules of the game. Prerequisite to this move was the construction of a boundaried space by the player; the move itself represented the materialization, the action, of that boundaried space. This action necessarily creates a boundaried space in the other player to which he can react in a number of ways—continue as if nothing extraordinary had happened, draw another row of squares to include the checker piece and resume the game, remove the piece, throw the board in the air, shake a fist in the face of the opponent, move his own pieces into imaginary spaces, begin moving all pieces two spaces instead of one, slap the opponent in the face, emit a cry of anguish, etc.

In other words, there exists a myriad array of possible *counteractions,* each outside the normal rules and strategies. Such counteractions entail "the modification (possibly the rejection)" of some form of knowledge possessed previously about rules and/or strategies. It requires that customary (and *condensed*) boundaried spaces be countered by slightly deviant to radically distinct boundaried spaces. Only by means of such *counterspaces* is it possible to re-cluster previous spaces; that is, to construct new classes and boundaries. But how often do checker players in seriousness engage in such metacommunication by means of *counterspaces?* Do they not customarily follow rather blindly and tacitly the conventional set of rules and try consciously to develop strategies?

Similarly, do we not tend to follow habitual speech patterns, pathways of least linguistic resistance, when speaking? And does our style not in many respects tend to crystallize as our writing becomes more habitual? The problem is that speaking and writing activities are at variance in a fundamental way. Speaking style is relatively spontaneous and nonconscious, while writing style can more easily be altered drastically by the self-conscious writer over a given period of time. In other words, to put marks-on-paper when writing is to construct material manifestations of boundaried spaces that can endure through time as a relatively static, crystallized system.[3] These marks can then relatively easily be countered by means of another set of marks. Marks and their respective countermarks can be critically compared and contrasted from within the domain of learning III such that the organization of subsequent marks represents the formation of yet new and distinct sets of boundaried spaces. On the other hand, spoken words are more closely tied to their context and they usually occur only once, except when embodied in rituals, myths, folktales, etc., or when recorded on a magnetic tape or some such device. Constituting a linear stream of messages, spoken words, given the obvious limitations of human memory, are not as readily susceptible to the same juxtaposition, comparison, and contrast as written texts.

We are about to reach the central core of this inquiry. Let us proceed to a discussion of marks—their material manifestations, their functions, and their purposes. Then we will be in a position to better understand the complementarity I have tentatively referred to between spoken and written language.[4]

Chapter 9
The Semiotic Web:
Our Chronic Prejudices

9.10 Preliminaries

9.11 Up to this point I have: (1) tentatively pointed out the direction for a theory of written signs, (2) integrated these foundations for a theory into prevalent views of human perception and cognition, and (3) constructed a hierarchical model of sign use that includes increasingly complex levels of consciousness and of learning, from the lower organisms to humans. The remaining task is to propose a concept of written texts that is commensurate with these views.

9.12 Let us now return to the beginning, but from yet another perspective, that of the material manifestations of boundaried spaces.

Observe a spider as it spins its web. It is constructing the materialization, the somewhat abstract externalization, of an inner boundaried space. Assume that the spider is not conscious of the purpose of its actions. (Perhaps much like the purposeless goal of the "Zen of archery.") It does it because it is innately programmed to do it. It follows a set of invariant rules (the code) and employs certain strategies depending upon the geographical terrain upon which it constructs its web.

Although invariant in design, this externalized boundaried space organizes a small part of the world. It is potentially information, it sends out messages to other aware or unaware organisms, and brings in messages to the spider. It represents part of life as a small organized island in the overriding inorganic sea of chaos: It is negentropy.

The web, like the bee's honeycomb, can be considered as an arbitrary sign insofar as there is no necessary relation between the externalized space and the potential information conveyed. On the other hand, in terms of function these are the most geometrically economical and the most practical physical constructions possible. Hence not only are such spaces signs, but they also perform a function. They are at once an abstraction and they serve a concrete purpose.

Assume that a fly unawaredly flies into the web. The fly, like the spider, is not conscious of the web's purpose. By an "innate release mechanism" it attempts to free itself, and in so doing sets up vibrations that are sensed by the spider. Another "innate mechanism" in the spider's nervous system sends it out to paralyze its prey and either store it for a future meal or take it back to its lair and consume it. A materialized space has brought about a physical change in the state of the world.

Unlike the web's natural arbitrariness, abstraction, function, and purpose, materializations of boundaried spaces as marks-on-paper are both natural and cultural, collective and individual, biological and psychological. For this reason such materializations are relatively amorphous, evolving through time. And, unlike the spider, the human being is at least partly conscious of the arbitrariness, abstraction, function, and purpose of his medium of communication and of the messages he emits.

9.13 With respect to the visual manifestation of boundaried spaces by means of writing, arbitrariness, abstraction, function, and purpose exist in degrees. For instance, in human cultures "writing" can occur in various forms: picture icons (the Aztecs), more-or-less arbitrary or allegorical figures (the Egyptians), picture-glyphs (the Mayans), cryptographs (the Chinese), or decomposition of words into elementary parts (Western world alphabetic writing). Notice that there is progression in this list of "writing" forms from relative concretion to abstraction, from nonarbitrariness to arbitrariness, from holistic or "analog" to "digital," and from "synthetic" to "analytic." Notice also that the alphabetic form exemplifies most explicitly the use of a ("digital") code by means of which to combine "bits" of meaningless signs into meaningful wholes, and that this code is relatively limited but offers the potential for generation of a limitless number of messages according to an array of different strategies.

Iconic forms represent only a minimal degree of abstraction since they are "analog" representations. They are relatively alinear and atemporal, the holistic manifestation of a conceptual whole. The space of the icon is analogous to the boundaried space, and both are analogous to the external material referent. From cryptographic to alphabetic writing, on the other hand, the signs themselves become increasingly abstract and less and less similar to the inner space and the outer referent; therefore they become increasingly arbitrary. Consequently, with alphabetic writing there can be increased explicitness with respect to the parts making up conceptual wholes. At the same time there tends to be a concomitant decreased awareness of the conceptual whole; spaces tend to become *condensed* and *embedment* inevitably follows. However, with increasing arbitrariness and abstraction, higher metalevels are possible as the medium is further removed from inner spaces and outer referents. Consequently, there exists the possibility of sending messages about those spaces and referents.[1]

Now let us see how increasingly complex metalevels are possible in human thought, and how they are embodied in messages, especially in the form of written texts.

9.20 Steps Toward an Interactionist View of Texts

9.21 Consider the alphabetic form of writing. Call the minimal unit, the letter, a *grapheme*. Call the combination of meaningless units into a meaningful whole the *word*. A word can represent a minimal boundaried space.

Call the combination of words into a meaningful evocation a *statement*. A boundaried space, as we shall see below, can be *condensed* so that it represents one or more statements. Or, a statement ordinarily represented by a *condensed* boundaried space can be reduced to a single word, as was the case of the above Wittgensteinian "thought experiments."

Finally, call the combination of a set of relatively coherent statements a *text*.[2] It is at times possible for an entire text to be *condensed* into a single boundaried space. Such a boundaried space might be called the "macrosemantic level" of the text (van Dijk, 1972), the text's "root metaphor" (Pepper, 1942), or the "sense" of the text (Vygotsky, 1962). It entails, if you will, a "Supericon."

9.22 A grapheme is a *mark*. It is a presence of or an absence of. The mark is a *figure* that must be distinguished from other marks in a word. This distinction is not presence/absence or figure/ground but *differentiation*. If the spider must be able to *differentiate* between meaningless and meaningful vibrations along the network of its web, the human organism must be able to *differentiate* between meaningless and meaningful marks in a word. A is easily *differentiable* as an "A" in the context of a word. But A → A → A → A become less and less so. The final set of marks might even in context be totally meaningless to some humans.

9.23 There are certain complementary relationships between boundaried spaces and their names (marks). Let us be mindful of these relationships before focusing on the *difference* between speech and writing.

Consider the minimal meaningful unit: the word. Mark off a space. Name (mark) the space x. Let the name (mark) become the same as the space. You now have: $\bigcirc \smile x \rightarrow \bigcirc\bigcirc$. Put the second space into the first space. This is the "same as" the space. Hence:

$$\bigcirc\bigcirc \rightarrow \circledcirc \rightarrow \bigcirc \text{ (by Axiom I)}.$$

Therefore:

$$\bigcirc \smile^{x} \rightarrow \bigcirc.$$

This is the "same as" the result of *embedment,* as described above, where the word is conceived/perceived to be the "real" thing, or the map the territory. In this case, what would ordinarily be conceived/perceived as direct intrinsic linkage between the boundaried space and the name is now erroneously conceived/perceived as absolute identity.

Now, consider this statement: "Billy Carter is loony." Let "Billy Carter" be x, the subject or name (set of marks). Let "is loony" be y, the predicate (set of marks). If you connect the words (marks) to their spaces, then you have:[3]

$$\bigcirc^{1} \smile x + \bigcirc^{2} \smile y = \bigcirc^{1} \smile x \bigcirc^{2} \smile y.$$

(Where the superscripts represent "subject space" and "predicate space" respectively.)

Combine the two spaces into a whole, just as concatenated words (marks) are combined into whole grammatically correct statements. You now have:[4]

This third "whole space" is the *condensation* of the first two spaces. It is also "more than the sum of its parts." That is, the first two spaces "interact" as combined concatenated parts to produce a *condensed* whole whose meaning is "more than" the sum of the meanings of the two parts in isolation. This is the "same as if" the two atomic parts (spaces) had been recrossed and then cancelled:

$\varnothing^1\varnothing^2 \rightarrow$ _____ (By AXIOM II, and by the *contraction* operation.)

And, since the meanings of the first and second spaces have been cancelled, upon their interaction, to produce a new meaning that is "more than" the sum of the first two meanings, then:

$$\varnothing^1\, \varnothing^2 \rightarrow \underline{\quad} \rightarrow \bigcirc\!\!\bigcirc^3 .$$

Or in other words:

$$\varnothing^1\, \varnothing^2 \rightarrow \bigcirc\!\!\bigcirc^3 .$$

According to AXIOMS III and IV, it can be stated that: $xy\, xy = xy$, and, $xy + \text{not } xy =$ _____. Hence, if from the above.

$$\underline{\quad} \rightarrow \bigcirc\!\!\bigcirc^3 .$$

and, $xy + \text{not } xy =$ _____, then:

$$xy + \text{not } xy = \underline{\quad} \rightarrow \bigcirc\!\!\bigcirc^3 .$$

Or in other words:

$$xy + \text{not } xy = \bigcirc\!\!\bigcirc^3 .$$

That is, the statement (set of marks) has been erroneously conceived/ perceived as the "real" space (or potentially as the "real" thing).[5]

9.24 In general, the successive *condensation* of spaces as described in the preceding section accompanies an increase of nonconsciousness of wholes, of "analog" images (or of belief systems and world views). And an increase in this nonconsciousness of wholes entails *embedment* of spaces and ultimately diminished attention to the parts within those wholes. Conversely, increasing consciousness of parts within wholes by reconstruction and recall of previously *embedded* spaces demands increased consciousness of those wholes (see Polanyi, 1958).

However, a certain degree of tacit or nonconscious awareness is always necessary. Specific attention to all the parts within a whole on a simple one-thing-at-a-time basis would be uneconomical, unproductive. Even computers and rats are programmed to be smarter than ` that. Expectations or hypotheses, as described above, entail tacit awareness of broad "analog" images. These expectations or hypotheses, through habituation, become *embedded* in consciousness such that what is expected or what is hypothesized to be the case is perceived on a broad level and within a specific context. Many of the particulars are consequently perceived little or not at all. Hence, like the embedded spaces discussed in 7.48, *condensation* of spaces entails tacit awareness of broad conceptual frameworks. It follows, then, that *condensed* spaces, at the deepest levels, constitute sets of nonconscious expectations and hypotheses (or beliefs) that can come to function in much the same way as "innate" knowledge (see, for example, the works of Bateson, 1972; Butler, 1913; Peirce, 1960; Polanyi, 1958; Schrödinger, 1945).

In the next sections we shall see how graphemic texts offer the most effective means by which spaces can be *de-embedded*.

9.25 There is a *difference* between oral cultures, in which knowledge is conveyed through speech, and literate cultures, in which explicit knowledge can be conveyed primarily through written texts.[6] In literate cultures all information need not be carried around in the head in neuronal and mnemonic networks, to be recreated and reinvented with each new time period and with each new generation. The networks are in a sense recorded as marks-on-paper (or as programs in a computer), and the knowledge they embody is transmitted by relatively explicit instruction; it is not learned by imitation but by formal training.[7]

What does this observation imply for literate cultures? Consider the following:

(a) The written marks (graphemes) making up texts establish boundaries, categories, distinctions, classes, and frames to a considerably greater degree than utterances. Notions of distinct beginnings and endings, of oppositions and identities, of contradictions and excluded middles, are forthcoming. From these notions Western world thought processes appear to be the "logical" result. (After all, what would become of symbolic logic, algebra, or the calculus, if we no longer enjoyed the possibility of visualizable graphemes?) (Goody, 1977).

(b) Written texts, as the partial and incomplete material manifestations of boundaried spaces, endure over time in a relatively static sense in contrast to the relatively dynamic and amorphous nature of utterances (speech). Consequently, there exists a greater possibility for abstracting particular sentences, words, and graphemes from a text.

(c) When written texts are broken down into isolated segments, those segments can then be relatively easily juxtaposed, compared, and contrasted. That is, they can be subjected to analysis by means of which consciousness of parts, and eventually consciousness of *condensed* and *embedded* wholes, can be increased.

(d) Unlike traditional oral cultures where words are relatively tightly bound up into the things they represent, words in written texts can be viewed more objectively, and with a greater degree of detachment—although, as we observed above, the tendency to equate words with things invariably persists. By means of such relative detachment and through the principles briefly outlined in (a)-(c), modern individuals, by writing and reading texts, can with greater facility become skeptical of their expectations, hypotheses, beliefs. Then they are prepared for reception of new ideas.

(e) Although as Goody (1977) maintains, a principal "distinctive feature" between traditional cultures and literate cultures seems to consist of "oral complexity" versus "graphic simplicity," graphic manifestations of boundaried spaces are never so concise as desired. Graphic modes of classification are always to a degree arbitrary, incomplete, and many times inconsistent. In order to patch up inconsistencies that appear in a given community's classificatory scheme, new subboundaries, subtaxonomies, subframes, subcategories, etc., must always be constructed. Consequently the scheme tends to evolve toward an increasing state of complexity; that is, until a new world is "seen" from within the domain of the higher level learning III by a given individual in that community. Subsequently, if that individual (a scientist, philosopher, seer, revolutionary, etc.) is successful in "converting" the community to this new world, ordered simplicity is reestablished. And the process begins anew.[8]

(f) Literate cultures, especially Western world cultures with phonetic writing, tend to develop predominantly linear, context-free, and relatively explicit communicative modes, in contrast to oral cultures whose communication is relatively nonlinear, context-dependent, and implicit. Yet the opposite but complementary mode always exists in each culture; it is always present partly at conscious and partly at tacit levels (with respect to such complementarity, see Bateson, 1972; Watzlawick, 1977; Watzlawick, Weakland, Fisch, 1974).

9.26 It might appear from the foregoing that literate cultures enjoy a tremendous advantage over oral cultures. Yes and no. *Yes,* because on perceiving speech representation, the mind must trust memory. The impossibility of recalling everything that preceded a given set of uttered statements renders the mind relatively incapable of perceiving category mistakes, ambiguities, contradictions, and paradoxes (see Lévi-Strauss, 1963, on anomaly at "unconscious levels" in all myths). However, *no,* since if all organisms search constantly for regularities, the limitations of memory on the individuals in an oral culture allow for a remarkable degree of security; that is, in the oral tradition regularities may be more easily perceived, and hence category mistakes, ambiguities, contradictions, and paradoxes are not so readily apparent. On the other hand, *yes,* for the *differentiated* characteristic of graphemes and the graphemic code offers multiple possibilities, and potentially, therefore, there can be a greater degree of change, of *organizational complexity* (see COROLLARY I, 1.36). The graphemic text, upon being reviewed, recalled, deconstructed, and reconstructed, opens itself more easily to reveal human error of thought. Human fallibilism becomes more readily evident, as category mistakes, ambiguities, contradictions, and paradoxes are discovered. Although throughout this process a degree of security is lost, the advantage is that critical analysis of graphemic texts repeatedly opens them up to resolution, to improvement, to development. And such critical analysis demands increasingly complex metalevels of awareness by means of learning III. However, the advantage is only ephemeral, for from within these metalevels new problems, ambiguities, contradictions, and paradoxes inevitably arise.

9.27 (An epistemological aside.) The reader might have perceived at this point that ultimately the model I am constructing seems to imply a materialistic form of reductionism. That is, what I have said implies that consciousness is presumably the nonmaterial aspect of thought processes that, like the relationship of the wave function to the particle function of light or matter, is complementary to the brain where the material aspect of thought processes occurs (and where they might eventually be studied empirically). In this sense the brain becomes a vast conglomerate of atoms and molecules, and these atoms and molecules, through their nonmaterial projection, are able to interpret marks-on-paper that are themselves collections of atoms and molecules that were placed there by the nonmaterial projection of another conglomerate of atoms and molecules; that is, of another brain. The circle appears to be vicious. Not so. It is open.

Modern quantum mechanics has abolished the notion of isolatable objects and has introduced the concept of the scientist as a "participator" in events rather than as an "observer" of them (for some earlier statements see Heisenberg, 1958; Bohr, 1958). Ultimately, it appears necessary to include human consciousness in any viable description of a given aspect of the world since the universe is now conceived as an interconnected web of physical and mental relations, the parts of which are definable only by virtue of their connections with the whole (Wigner, 1970). If nonmaterial "consciousness" is to be an essential aspect of future theories of matter (including the brain), then just as wave functions are not separable from but complementary to particle functions, so human consciousness is not separable from but complementary to the brain. And, just as in quantum mechanics the ultimate question was: "What are these waves waves of?", so the ultimate question with respect to human thought processes and the generation of boundaried spaces may be: "What is the consciousness consciousness of?"

Already this question entails its concomitant metaquestion. Already the system is opened. To ask the question is to be conscious that there is something$_1$ that possesses consciousness of something$_2$. Something$_2$ is part of an interconnected whole that includes the consciousness of something$_1$ and that is unintelligible outside that whole. The fact that something$_1$ that is ultimately a conglomerate of atoms and molecules can be conscious of itself and of something$_2$ that is another conglomerate of atoms and molecules is amazing, yet still a fact. And, like the constantly expanding universe, this system is perpetually expanded to include higher levels and broader contexts (for a masterful demonstration of the brain-mind relationship, though on certain issues I do not agree totally with his view, see Hofstadter, 1979).

In the section that follows I begin discussion of a model with which to account for the possibility of such expansion by way of increasingly complex metaleveled boundaried spaces. Then I will attempt to demonstrate that this expansion is most adequately attained through *written texts:* sets of *graphemes.*

9.30 Why Do We Write/Read Texts?

9.31 Bühler (1934) proposes three functions for a language:

(a) *Expressive:* The message must serve to express the emotions or thoughts of the language user.

(b) *Signaling* or *stimulative:* The message stimulates a certain response in the addressee.

(c) *Descriptive:* The message describes a particular state of affairs.

To these three functions, Popper (1963, 1972) adds a fourth:

(d) *Argumentative* or *explanatory:* presentation of alternative thoughts, views, or propositions to descriptive or expressive messages as defined in (c).

Let (a) through (d) be submitted as potentially viable propositions for the present inquiry.

9.32 Clearly, (a), (c), and (d) can be isolated in terms of output while (b) entails input and corresponding behavior; hence I will bracket out (b) for the present. What follows will project Bühler's and Popper's terminology into a larger classificatory scheme.

Let (a) consist of the class of nonverbal human and animal messages. This class includes auditory cries and signals that are: (1) holistic and continuous (most animals, and human exclamations), (2) composed of the combination of arbitrary parts and hence discontinuous and "digital" (bird whistles, words in human natural and artificial languages), or (3) both "analog" and "digital" (the bee dance, human language looked at from the context of sentences and texts) (Masters, 1970; Sebeok, 1972). Whether "analog," "digital," or a mixture of the two modes, expressive messages are invariably the materialization of continuous boundaried spaces.

Let (c) consist of statements or propositions formulated in human natural or artificial languages by means of the combination of graphemes or other symbolic forms into "digitalized" sequences that can and usually do represent continuous boundaried spaces. In this sense, (c) can also consist of visual, auditory, and verbal art forms (sculpture, painting, music, prose and poetry, film) as well as scientific models and sketches, diagrams, graphs, and maps, which manifest both "analog" and "digital" characteristics.

9.33 In light of the preceding, two definitions follow:

(I) Descriptive messages can be: (i) chiefly implicit, in the case of visual or auditory art forms (painting, sculpture, music, etc.); (ii) implicit and explicit, in the case of verbal art forms (poetry, which is usually more implicit than explicit, and prose, which may be more explicit than implicit) or art forms that combine verbal and visual (drama, film, etc.); (iii) chiefly explicit, in the case of linguistically formulated statements with the purpose of informing, convincing, instructing, etc.; or (iv) chiefly explicit, in the case of scientific models and sketches, diagrams, graphs, and maps.

(II) Sophisticated animal forms of communication border on the descriptive mode.

Implicit descriptive messages sent and received on partly tacit levels are predominantly of "analog" character. Explicit descriptive messages break up a state of affairs into constituent parts, hence they are less tacit and sent and received as discontinuous ("digitalized") parts of a continuous boundaried space. Predominantly implicit descriptive messages tend to be more *condensed* in nature. Predominantly explicit descriptive messages tend to be less *condensed* in nature.

Descriptive messages within human communicative systems presuppose, from particular perspectives, truth-values, belief, doubt, skepticism, and so on. Therefore they must implicitly or explicitly convey what is considered to be "truth" or "falsity," belief, doubt, skepticism, etc., about something or in support of or in reaction to some situation or state of affairs. In this sense, a descriptive message is necessarily an expressive message insofar as it is the outward manifestation of some internal thought, emotion, or attitude. It also performs a signaling or stimulative function since it is capable of provoking a negative or positive response.

9.34 With respect to Popper's linguistic function, two more definitions follow:

(III) Argumentative or explanatory messages are: (i) the manifestation of agreement or opposition to some other descriptive or argumentative message; and (ii) the implicit or explicit, and tacit or conscious formulation of reasons, whether intuitive, intellectual or emotive, for such agreement or opposition.

(IV) The argumentative mode is uniquely human.

Argumentative messages consist of well-formulated scientific theories explaining a descriptive model, analyses of art works, or explanations of general hypotheses, concepts, and opinions with the intention of convincing the addressee. The messages can be appropriately about descriptive messages, hence they are necessarily derived from particular and rather well-defined perspectives about "truth" or "falsity," belief, doubt, skepticism, etc. They are also about problems inherent in descriptive messages.

For instance, consider the following:

(a) Biting rats can be fatal (ambiguity).

(b) Jack is tall and consists of four letters (category mistake).

(c) This statement is false (contradiction).

(d) All cats are mortal.

Socrates is mortal.

Therefore, Socrates is a cat (false reasoning: inconsistent conclusions from consistent premises).

All four of these statements can be perceived merely as descriptive messages. In this sense, they could be sent by an addresser who is unaware that they can be interpreted in different ways or interpreted not at all by the addressee. On the other hand, to explain their inadequacy and to argue for alternative messages capable of avoiding these inadequacies entails the generation of complementary messages of a different level, a metalevel. That is, it requires awareness of the problem situations inherent in the messages. Hence in order for the addresser to clarify his messages he must first discover the problems inherent in them. Then he can attempt to resolve these problems by talking or thinking about the messages.

9.35 *Expressive messages* are characteristically "dogmatic"; that is, closed. There is little or no possibility, within the framework of these messages, of opening the system and moving to a metalevel. The rudiments of a metalevel are apparent in, for instance, animal play activity, but the system is rarely opened. In human play and games, a breach of the closed system of rules is certainly possible but at the expense of talking about those rules; that is, of using descriptive or argumentative messages. Expressive messages pertain appropriately to learning I since they involve signals, indexical denotation, and, with respect to human language, naming.

Descriptive messages entail taxonomies of signals, indexes, names. Systems of descriptive messages can relatively easily be breached (even the "talking apes" supposedly do it) to create new classes. However, these messages are evocative: There is no or little possibility for counterargument or discussion about the validity of a system of classification. Consequently, when an organism's use of a particular mode of classificatory signs becomes habitual, its system is closed and its habits of thought tend toward "dogmatism." Learning II occurs within this system but the rules tend to become relatively fixed and the number of strategies is reduced. With a breach of the system and subsequent new classificatory schemes, the rules and strategies undergo alteration, but invariably they once again tend to become fixed.

Argumentative messages entail the comparative juxtaposition of two or more sets of descriptive messages. However, they can be either closed and "dogmatic" or open and critical. From the closed perspective, argument is from within the system of only one of the juxtaposed messages or sets of messages. From the open or metaperspective, argument critically evaluates both. Learning II occurs within the closed system argumentative mode and learning III is possible from within the open system argumentative mode. Learning III necessarily entails an absence of fixed strategies and rules since at the instant when the act of creation-invention-discovery occurs within the realm of learning III, there can be ideally no system. However, when a perspective is subsequently selected, rules and strategies are inevitably established.

It is apparent, in light of the above discussion that: EXPRESSIVE MODE $\subseteq$ DESCRIPTIVE MODE $\subseteq$ ARGUMENTATIVE MODE. However, higher levels of communication are not "nothing but" special cases of the lower levels; human languages are not "nothing but" sophisticated animal languages. Moreover, it is not the case here that the distinction between human and animals is not a matter of degree but of kind. The distinction is both of degree and kind, depending upon the perspective. I will attempt to illustrate this assertion in the following sections.

9.36 A "thought experiment" in part derived from Popper (1963, 296-97):

A thermostat "expresses" its internal state and it can even be said to "signal" and to "describe" it, since it consists in the continuous ("analog") movement of a pointer along a graduated ("digital") scale that causes a circuit to switch ("digitally") on or off at a particular point. In other words, since it is a mixture of "analog" and "digital" systems it is capable of generating a description of a particular aspect of the external state of affairs. However, responsibility for such description is not attributed to the machine but to its maker. It does not of itself describe any more than does a typewriter, a bicycle, or a car.

Now, consider a more complex machine with a built-in lens, a language analyzer, and an apparatus for duplicating speech. Whenever one of a set of objects is placed before the lens the machine names it, or it may say, if it has not been programmed for that object, "I don't know." It is also programmed to respond to questions like, "What color is this book?" or, "How many balls are there?" And it can generate its own messages describing internal states such as, "I don't like that color," "Those balls are ugly," "I'm tired, let's stop," or, "Please talk to me." Even though the behavior of this machine can become very much like that of a human there is in principle no fundamental difference between the thermostat and this "observing" and "describing" machine. It has been "programmed," like the "conditioning" of a human or an animal, to respond to certain stimuli without any concomitant *intention* to describe; it is merely the expression of signals.

Blindfold a small child, place him in front of this machine with a set of the above-mentioned objects, and tell him to talk to it. The child may easily be led to believe that he is communicating with a human being. He may even believe that the machine is "describing" and even "arguing" like a human. In other words, from his perspective we might infer that the distinction between man and machine, or between man and animal, is of degree. Nevertheless, for the maker of the machine its behavior may be no more mysterious than the functioning of a thermostat or a clock. That is, when the causal behavior of the machine is known, there is the realization that it is only capable of purely expressive and signaling functions. From the perspective of the machine's maker, then, it cannot be endowed with human capacities: The distinction is in kind. In other words, nature, viewed from the perspective of culture, is opposed to it; culture, from the perspective of nature, is also an incommensurable domain. But nature *and* culture, whether viewed intellectually from a metalevel, or perceived intuitively, form a continuum of values. Yet we invariably tend to impute cultural capacities in other human beings as if nature and culture were a dichotomy. What are the implications of this tendency?

9.37 If we convey descriptive messages to other people and argue with them we tacitly assume that they are able to comprehend our descriptions and our arguments and perhaps to generate counterarguments. We know by experience that we have intentions and we assume the same in other people. We possess truth-values, beliefs, doubts, skepticism, and we presuppose that others do also. If we can constantly become aware of previously concealed problems and attempt to remedy them by the application of a wide range of alternative solutions we believe that those with whom we communicate can do the same. If we are perpetually capable of breaching our systems of thought and of sign use we expect others to possess a comparable ability (however, for the problems inherent in this "reasoning by analogy," see Malcolm, 1971).

Do humans or can humans seriously and adequately argue with machines or apes? Or better, do they ordinarily even bother trying? The so-called "talking apes" are taught by humans; let us not forget this important fact. They are in a sense "programmed" by a non-ape organism to "speak" like that organism speaks (Marler, 1977). By use of this non-ape "language" it appears that the apes have, perhaps, demonstrated a certain degree of creativity; indeed all animals are to a degree creative. Perhaps we can even say that there must be some very limited degree of "intention" directing their behavior—although, we must assume, whether these "intentions" are at conscious or nonconscious levels cannot be known with certainty. If not, the responses of animals of the same species would always be the same, like two identical thermostats or two identical "players" of a von Neumannian game; animals are not "nothing but" machines.

Yet, neither is the human "nothing but" a talking ape. The distinction is automatically made, even by those who are attempting to refute Chomsky and dissolve the nature/culture dichotomy. Hence, the dichotomy is not real, but artificial. And yet, it is real, for in order that the ape effectively argue by use of its non-ape language it must be able to talk about that language, at the argumentative level. It must be capable of comparing its own ape form of communication with the non-ape language "programmed" into it by humans. It must be able to argue about the truth-value of descriptive messages conveyed through that language, and to do so it must be capable of belief, doubt, skepticism, and so on. In addition, it must respond to such relatively simple but value-laden statements as, "Eating caviar is more cultured than eating bananas." Such responses involve comparative judgments rather than relatively static taxonomies, and they involve attention to vague and ambiguous areas that invariably lead to alterations of established taxonomies. It must also eventually be capable of such statements as: "Would you please repeat your last statement, I didn't understand it," or, "You are lying," or, "I believe that you are wrong for the following reasons:. . . ." These sentences entail nonvoluntary modes of thought derived from belief, doubt, skepticism, etc. They are ultimately impossible without the capacity of the organism for learning III.

In sum, learning III and the argumentative mode, of which the human is capable with relative facility, is only accessible to the more intelligent animals at the most rudimentary level. There is, then, a nature/culture dichotomy, and there is not, depending upon the eye of the beholder. This point bears further discussion.

Chapter 10

Text and Countertext

10.10 "Thought Experiments": Steps toward a Typology of Countermessages

10.11 A bat in a cave sends out auditory signals with the "expectation" of receiving information from its environment. Its sophisticated "sonar" system keeps it informed in such a way that it can maneuver in this relatively small enclosed area at high speeds without colliding with the walls of the cave. It can be stated that the organism emits signals and receives *countersignals* that it is genetically equipped to interpret by means of a fixed set of rules (see the countersignals discussed in 1.27).

The bat "checks" these countersignals against its original squeak, and the *differences* between the two tells it how far it is from the walls of the cave, from another flying bat, or from an insect. If the bat detects an insect it begins to close in on the messages denoting "food." As it approaches the insect the *differences* between the two frequencies—the emitted squeak and the echo—diminish. When the *differences* become very small it opens its mouth and eats the "echo"; that is, what *was* the echo, since at the point where the message (echo) becomes nonexistent the denotatum of that message (echo) becomes real—(the bat is in this sense wiser than most humans since it never confuses the name with the thing named, or the boundaried space with the name). Note the important fact that countersignals are necessarily perceived as *differences*.

10.12 Each member in a flock of geese flying overhead repeatedly emits "honks" and receives what appears to be the same message as a sort of countersignal from its neighbors. These messages might denote, "Here I am," or "Keep your distance," or some such thing. By this cybernetic-like system of constant feedback these geese are able to maneuver in unison, maintaining approximately the same distance between one another (Count, 1969). Each goose's message, like the bat's exploratory signals, is met by what might be called counter-signals from other geese, which serve to inform it, by means of *differences* in sound frequencies and loudness, concerning its position relative to the flock.

10.13 The bee that emits the wrong scent on entering the hive sends out messages that are potentially "expected" but that are counter to the messages that would ordinarily be received under "normal" circumstances. A radical *difference*, or a rudimentary form of negation, exists with respect to these countersignals. They also represent a primitive form of metacommunication. There is little chance for confusion. However, as a communicative system becomes more complex, confusion can arise out of the possibility of *countermessages* that contradict or negate other countermessages that could potentially be sent out in the same context.

For example, I kick a sleeping dog. The animal can respond in a number of ways to my "unexpected" message that represents a *difference* with respect to what would ordinarily be expected. If the dog feels it can take me on and if it is in an ill mood it might jump up and bite me. This countersignal existed within the range of my expectations, even though the dog's response was low on my probability list. I am in for a fight.

10.14 An ape has many tokens to "talk" with. Assume that among them are tokens for "round," "fruit," and "ball." The ape is given a new item that it has never before experienced, such as, say, a small melon. This object lies beyond its range of "expectations." Yet in spite of the *difference* between this new item of experience and all other objects the ape might have "expected," there are certain similarities between it and what some of the ape's tokens represent. Hence the *differences* are less than those of the dog, the geese, the bees, or the bat example. Yet these *differences* make a meaningful *difference*. There exists a certain sameness and at the same time there is *difference*, not opposition but just *difference*, which provides for similarities.

What can the ape do? It can "name" the new object with any of the three tokens by way of the similarity between what they represent and the melon. Or it can silently throw the melon against the wall or try to eat it. It may also give it back to the owner, show disinterest, and so on. In whichever case, there exists a relatively large range of possible responses to the new situation. But the important point is that each response entails the prior perception of *difference.*

10.15 Now, examples 10.11-10.14 involve the *expressive* and *signaling* functions discussed above. Expressive countersignals within the domain of human communication include paralinguistic messages, naming, moans, grunts, exclamations, etc. The function of such countersignals, like animal forms of countersignals, remains at a low level of effectiveness. There can be no more than a rudimentary mode of negation, and there is certainly no way to actively and critically compare, contrast, or give reasons. There can be an intent on the part of the addresser to convince the addressee of the validity of the countersignal only in a more-or-less "analog" fashion: the emphasis of a groan when in pain, the force of a kick, the intensity of a facial expression, and so on.

Nevertheless, this rudimentary form of negation, such as that discussed in 1.27, possesses the same negative qualities as metaphorization and metonymization. "Unexpected" countersignals "say" what ordinarily would not be the case, and therefore response to these countersignals is something other than what it would ordinarily be.

10.20 Higher Countermessages

10.21 At the level of the *descriptive* function, a statement or proposition explicitly formulated in a natural language can be countered with an equal and opposite descriptive statement or proposition without stating reasons for giving justifications, or for establishing a basis for explicit comparison. One statement or proposition is simply juxtaposed with another statement or proposition. For example, in communicating with an ape by use of non-ape language, one might generate the command, "You scratch me," which could be met with the countercommand, "*You* scratch *me.*" At an exceedingly more complex level, the scientific proposition, "The earth is the center of the universe," could simply be countered with, "The sun is the center of the universe." Or, in the case of a poetic text, a few of Thomas More's moralistic lines:

> The first point is to love but one alone,
> And for that one all other to forsake:
> For whoso loveth many loveth none.

could be juxtaposed with a few ribald lines from *The Book of Good Love* by the Arcipreste de Hita.

These descriptive *counterstatements* and *counterpropositions* can implicitly convey beliefs, faith, doubt, certainty, skepticism, and so on, without there being the immediate need to talk about them. Value judgments are possible with respect to the referents of these statements and propositions, but judgment concerning their validity pertains to another level. That is, there can be no discussion about conflicting theories, no analysis of works of art, no discussion concerning who is boss and who should give commands. The descriptive mode is simply limited to, in the linguistic sense, the sentential or subject-predicate portrayal of the emotive and conceptual content of the expressive mode.

Descriptive counterstatements or counterpropositions can be, especially in the case of art, chiefly implicit, while in science and other fields of inquiry explicitness is demanded. Nevertheless, in scientific model construction as well as in the arts, metaphor (that is, the figurative use of language) has proved to be perhaps the most effective and economical way to "show" the distinction between a statement and its counterstatement. The form of negation implicit in all metaphors is, as discussed above, an essential part of figurative language. By use of figurative language a new image is created that counters a conventionally held image. It suggests a new meaning, concept, or theory, and it potentially shows how the old conventional image was inadequate. This countermessage is what the message is all about. It is the core of the semiotic function of all novel messages in human languages. The syntactic structures of grammar rules of the natural language by means of which a countermessage is generated are not relevant here. What is important is the boundaried space and its materialization as opposed to other potential and actual boundaried spaces and their materialization.

Hence just as individual graphemes are relatively meaningless until integrated into words, and just as words are not adequately intelligible outside the context of sentences, so grammatically formed statements are not adequately intelligible in terms of their total semiotic function unless they are considered in light of other compatible statements within a given text, and in light of other statements with which they *differ* in other texts.

10.22 *Counterarguments* in *countertexts* generated by means of the *argumentative* function demand *reasons* and *justification*. Here counter-statements and counterpropositions are not merely juxtaposed, they are critically compared. In the process messages are generated about the underlying truth-values and beliefs of counterstatements and counterpropositions. The intent is to convince the reader that one theory, philosophy, technique, style, is better than another.

It was proposed above that all organisms possess a philosophy, whether they are aware of the fact or not. Given certain parameters of choice, narrow in the lower organism and potentially limitless over time for the human organism, there understandably exists preference for one thing or another, one idea or another. In this way, by a selec-tive trial-and-error process a given philosophy changes, is improved. If all adult males kick a dog every time they are near it, soon the dog will develop a "philosophy" of avoidance of adult males. But the dog has exercised relatively little power of choice and selection. Its "phi-losophy" is a defensive and selective, but relatively passive, response to its environment. It has not, we would assume, forayed out into its world actively in search of a better "philosophy," although it does go out into the world in the active sense in order to satisfy certain biolog-ical needs.

In contrast, as was pointed out above, the human animal is never completely satisfied with his philosophy. Each individual, to a greater or lesser degree, searches his intellectual environment in hopes of satisfying his curiosity about the world and of gratifying his need for an orderly universe. He incessantly tries out his philosophy (or hy-pothesis) on his environment, and if contradictions arise he attempts to resolve them by altering his philosophy or possibly by replacing it with another. These appendages to his philosophy are derived from the *counterexamples* he perceives and the counterarguments he gener-ates for himself, and if his philosophy is abandoned, it is because he has acquired faith in some *counterphilosophy*.

However, let us remember that Popper (1963, 1972) argues effec-tively that the lower animals always do this on a simple level and the higher animals on increasingly more complex levels in a natural way and without awareness of their so doing. In such cases all organisms are capable of generating at least primitive *counterphilosophies*. Perhaps we could say that this activity derives from an innate mechanism for survival. If it is indeed innate this aspect of the activity of all orga-nisms is not of crucial interest here and hence I see no need to belabor the point. But the intriguing singularity is—and this important point bears reiterating also—that *human beings have somehow learned to perform this activity consciously.* This is indeed worthy of inquiry. In the sections that follow I propose a model for such a level of consciousness.

10.23 Let us consider the notion that the descriptive and argumentative functions are more predominant in literate cultures than in oral cultures—though, of course, they are never entirely absent in the latter. Linear, context-free, and relatively explicit modes of communication, more prevalent in literate communities, lend themselves to analysis (attention to the parts of a whole on a linear one-at-a-time basis), criticism (relatively free of linguistic contexts), and counterarguments (by juxtaposition of concepts). And, partly in order to avoid the above-discussed limitations when using spoken language, the most effective means for presenting analyses, criticisms, and counterarguments is in written texts.

The descriptive and argumentative functions embodied in written language vary, depending upon the type of text and the disposition of the reader. At the fundamental level, texts are primarily a descriptive juxtaposition of contrasting perspectives. This entails the act of *showing* that a particular text contrasts with other texts rather than explicitly *stating* these contrasts and *arguing for* one of the texts and against the others. As texts become more and more explicitly (and consciously) formulated, critical comparison and reasoned argumentation begins to displace descriptive juxtaposition with the accompanying attempt to attain greater explanatory adequacy. Paradigms of these two forms of written texts exist in Western world societies chiefly in artistic and scientific activity.

Art, considered as a form of knowledge, is generally a *showing* rather than an explicit *telling*, although essayistic prose tends toward the other extreme (Kuhns, 1970). Objects, acts, and events are juxtaposed in unorthodox ways, with the interjection of irony, satire, paradox, allegory, etc., to demonstrate the counterposition of one text to another text or texts, to counterpose styles, concepts, attitudes, beliefs, or world views. Comprehension of artistic texts consequently rests partly at tacit and implicit levels. These are the levels of the intersubjective "form of life" in which all human beings to a greater or lesser degree participate.

At the other end of the spectrum, scientific texts entail the more-or-less explicit formulation of ideas, concepts, and even of attitudes, beliefs, and styles. These texts are more overtly analytical, critical, and argumentative (Feyerabend, 1975). And, they must be testable (or falsifiable) (Popper, 1959). Consequently, they are constructed/ perceived with greater detachment, since they are not an intrinsic part of the author's or reader's intersubjective "form of life." Yet they presuppose a community of intellectuals who possess their own partly intersubjectively derived beliefs, attitudes, and scientific world views (Kuhn, 1970; Polanyi, 1958). Thus, these texts are also partly comprehended at the tacit level from within a specialized subcultural "form of life."

This must be the case, for if we observe, from a historical vantage point, the periodically changing world views of Western science, we are forced to conclude that what was yesterday's "falsity" can be today's "truth," and what is today's "truth" can be tomorrow's "absurdity" or "myth." What is conceived and perceived to be the "real world," from within a particular cultural milieu at a particular time and place, could always be other than what it is. "Truth," within given "forms of life," could always have been something else. And such epistemological variation is, it must be admitted, relatively more accessible within literate cultures (see Merrell, 1980b).

However, the problem to which we must address ourselves is: What is the principal feature distinguishing knowledge derived from texts and knowledge assimilated in oral traditions? A conjecture: The distinction lies in greater awareness of *successive differentiation*, which leads to a progressive movement from relative simplicity to complexity (cf. COROLLARY I, 1.36).

10.24 As was suggested above, the first step in the "trial-and-error" method for improving a philosophy is to become aware of problems; that is, of category mistakes, contradictions, and paradoxes. "One of the things a philosopher may do, and one of those that may rank among his highest achievements, is to see a *riddle*, a *problem*, or a *paradox*, not previously seen by anyone else" (Popper, 1963, 184). This is even a more noteworthy achievement than resolving them. Riddles, problems, and paradoxes become manifest when we become aware of, critical of, and dissatisfied with our expectations, or when we become aware of contradictions in our "philosophy."

To attain this level of awareness it is necessary to have already moved into the area of argumentative communication, to be able to speculate on or talk about descriptive messages: This presupposes the capacity to potentially operate in the realm of learning III. Only after critical comparison, while temporarily exposed to this realm, can the imaginative creation of bold new artistic styles and techniques, philosophical views, and scientific theories be forthcoming. Then these insights must be conveyed by means of either descriptive or argumentative messages.

For instance, a unique metaphor, a conceptual construct, or a scientific model comes "in a flash" during a wild flight of imagination: This is the Archimedean "Eureka" effect, a "logic of discovery." However, metaphors, conceptual constructs, and models alone may *suggest* much, but they *explain* very little or nothing. The philosophical or literary insight is barren without its linguistic formulation, and a scientific analogical model is inadequate unless dressed in theoretical language (Hanson, 1958, 1965; Toulmin, 1974). This second activity, the linguistic formulation of an original insight, constitutes what might be called a "logic of descriptive discourse" or a "logic of inferential reasoning." The former can be a countertext by *implying* distinctions between itself and other texts. The latter demands that a relatively explicit argument or counterargument be set up in a text that is adequately intelligible only with respect to other arguments and other texts.

By use of the descriptive mode accompanied by the argumentative mode, we conceive/perceive all texts to be *different* while at the same time we are invariably aware of something in them that is supposedly unchanged. This dual-level awareness must be the case. For if a given text were totally *different* from (i.e., opposed to) all other texts it would be unintelligible; if the same as all other texts it would be uninteresting. Dual-level awareness, by means of the "oscillatory model" described above, is precisely the recognition in a text of something unexpected (that is, awareness of that which is other than what ordinarily would have been the case). However, the awareness I refer to is not that of the ape's "awareness" when presented a melon. Proper awareness of *differences* through sameness and similarity with respect to counterdescriptive and counterargumentative texts requires a disposition toward a greater or lesser degree of skepticism, doubt, belief, etc. That is, it presupposes the ability to construct/perceive counter-countertexts. And this ability entails a relatively sophisticated degree of the analytical, critical, and argumentative modes.

10.25 Moreover, just as there can be no totally distinct and incommensurable texts, so there can be no such thing as two identical texts. Borges (1964) tells the story of Pierre Menard, whose ambition was to write a contemporary *Don Quixote;* not just another *Don Quixote* but *the Don Quixote:*

> The first method he conceived was relatively simple. Know Spanish well, recover the Catholic faith, fight against the Moors or the Turk, forget the history of Europe between the years 1602 and 1918, *be* Miguel de Cervantes. Pierre Menard studied this procedure . . . but discarded it as too easy. . . . To be, in the twentieth century, a popular novelist of the seventeenth seemed to him a diminution. To be, in some way, Cervantes and reach the *Quixote* seemed less arduous to him—and, consequently, less interesting—than to go on being Pierre Menard and reach the *Quixote* through the experiences of Pierre Menard.

Menard partially completed this latter "almost impossible" task in a fragment of *Don Quixote* that word for word was identical to part of the work of Cervantes. However, it was at the same time "more subtle" and "infinitely richer" than the original work. Menard's ability to capture a seventeenth-century foreign tongue, his recapitulation of thought that was no longer in general thought in the twentieth century but that nevertheless revealed the influence of Nietzsche, Russell, and James, and his ability to, unlike Cervantes, counterpose two unrealities rather than juxtapose the real with the irreal, clearly demonstrated Menard's "superiority" over Cervantes. Menard, we are told, completely renovated the rudimentary art of reading.

Of course, for the aware reader Menard's text is linguistically identical to but yet vastly *different* from Cervantes' text because their circumstances were radically distinct. To read Menard's text is in a sense like placing one's foot in the same river twenty years after having put it there the first time. The second text is a countertext even though it is a duplication of the first text. It tells us the same in the same words but reveals infinitely more because the semiotically derived boundaried spaces, which necessarily include texts, countertexts, and contexts, are at variance. Moreover, its countertextual characteristics are dependent upon the reader who, aware of the texts of both Cervantes and Menard, can speak about them. Otherwise Menard's text would be like the bug at the precise moment it enters the bat's mouth. It would not even be an "echo" of Cervantes' text. It would be that text itself.

10.26 Notice that I have reiterated the term *difference*. Understanding this term is crucial to understanding the nature of all texts (for further discussion of this term in somewhat the same way as I use it here, see Bateson, 1972, 1977). Even though the marks-on-paper are identical with respect to Menard's and Cervantes' texts, the contexts of the two writings and hence of the two proper readings *differ*. *Difference* in this sense is not material. It does not lie in the marks-on-paper or, from the above example, in the space between those marks and the eye of the conceiver/perceiver, nor does it lie between the bat and the walls. Nor can it be placed in time. To locate *difference* in time and space would be like the snapshot of a race car in action. It would be to posit a world incapable of change: Zeno's paradox.

Difference, then, *lies in the message as it is conceived/perceived.* It exists in boundaried spaces whose existence in time and whose conception/perception by way of their material manifestations in space can only be described by the oscillatory model. *Difference* is neither "inside" nor "outside" but nonparadoxically conceived/perceived as simultaneously both. It is neither of continuous nor discontinuous nature but at once both. Moreover, *difference*, like metaphor, always implies the existence of something that might otherwise be absent. The bat responds to an "echo" because it "knows" the "non-echo" is not there. The dog responds to a nip in the absence of a bite because it "knows" the relationship between nips and bites, and it "knows" that without the existence of the bite the nip would not represent a *difference:* Therefore it would be "meaningless." The chimp responds to a few plastic tokens on a board because it "knows" that their combination (message) represents for it a *difference* with respect to all other possible combinations (messages), and at the same time that these tokens represent a *difference* with respect to what their combination denotes.[1]

All counterstatements, counterpropositions, counterarguments, and countertexts are sums of *differences*. That is to say, they are the manifestation of sets of boundaried spaces that constitute a set of *differences* with respect to what otherwise might have been manifested. And these sets of boundaried spaces were originally activated by other *differences*, by messages that were conceived/perceived in a way other than the way they might ordinarily have been conceived/perceived. The question at this point is: How can these countertendencies arise and how do they become an ongoing process? Let me begin with an extension of the above comparison between oral cultures and literate cultures.

10.27 Imagine that we live in a culture that has not yet invented writing. We are a toolmaking people. In the absence of writing, our tools represent the most notable example of an exosomatic extension of our minds to be found in our culture. Our tools are ours and they exist as physical objects in contiguity with all other objects in our world. We see them, we use them, we discover better and better ways of making them, and consequently we never cease to improve on them.

The animals, like us, have rudimentary forms of exosomatic development. Beavers build dams, birds build nests, some birds "learn" to use sticks to get at insects in their holes, in captivity Köhler's apes have been able to "invent" primitive tools to obtain food, and so on. Our vast superiority over the animals is in part due to the fact that we have relatively advanced tools that have enhanced our biologically endowed capacities. Instead of learning to run faster to catch our prey we invented the bow and arrow. Instead of developing a heavy coat of fur we learned how to build houses. Instead of growing monstrous incisors to cut down trees we constructed crude axes. And so on.

Our superiority is also due to the fact that we have a language with which we can talk easily about the tools and hence better perceive their good points as well as their flaws; our tools are as a result in a constant state of evolution. But this evolution occurs at a relatively slow rate. Since nobody in our culture has invented writing, there have been no books written about our tools, weapons, or houses, nor are there any plans or blueprints. Communication about these tools is by word of mouth, and it must be passed on from generation to generation. As a consequence our tools change only slightly over time. Why is this?

The lack of radical change in our tools is comparable to the lack of any change, perceptible for us at least, in our myths. A priest reiterates at the appropriate festival one of our traditional legends. We have heard it all before, and we have even committed much or most of the "plot" to memory, but the details are vague. We derive a collective pleasure from re-listening to this charming tale. Since certain details are not clear in our minds we are sometimes not aware that the priest, having reiterated the myth from his own memory in the absence of a sacred script, has made a few changes, some unknowingly and some perhaps intentionally. Given our memory limitations, a portion of what we listened to at the beginning of the myth is not now available for immediate recall, hence we may be unaware of contradictions and inconsistencies in it. We are not able to compare and contrast statements in the myth in a graphic way as we could were we to possess written texts. And we certainly do not usually argue about these contradictions and inconsistencies nor about the validity of the myth. *Comparative juxtaposition* and *analysis,* then, are relatively unknown in our culture.

On the other hand, we do operate at the level of *taxonomies.* Our entire culture is an elaborate system of *classifications* (see Lévi-Strauss, 1966). Our messages consequently tend toward the *descriptive* mode and away from the *argumentative* mode. We attempt to mirror our environment rather than question it; we tend to be *bricoleurs* (taxonomists) rather than engineers (system builders); we live in our world rather than setting ourselves apart from it and imposing ourselves on it (Lévi-Strauss, 1966). Hence, when listening to our myth we usually remain, so to speak, "inside" it and "inside" our culture. Our existence takes on importance within the whole, rather than the whole for us. In short, the system of which we are a part is not frequently "opened" such that, from a metalevel, changes can be made.[2]

10.28 Hence the conjecture: *Counterstatements, counterexamples, counterarguments,* and *countertexts* (all of which are included within the general domain of *countersignal systems*) are less prevalent in oral than in literate cultures.

Does this imply that knowledge accumulation can occur most effectively in literate cultures? Is the incessant quest for truth that so adequately characterizes Western thought relatively absent in oral cultures?

Consider Peirce's concept of the growth of knowledge. For Peirce all thinking is necessarily with signs. But no thought is self-sufficient nor self-confirmatory; all thoughts require other thoughts to make them clear, and these thoughts in turn require others. Hence there is no knowledge (system of thought) that is not mediated by prior knowledge (systems of thought) (Peirce, 1958, 7.337). Only through this constant mediatory process can human knowledge grow. Such a mediatory process can certainly occur in oral cultures also. For example, the work of Lévi-Strauss (especially, 1969) seems to bear this out. The myths of the American Indians he studies represent an interwoven fabric of intertextuality, the complexity of which is surely comparable to the literary tradition of many, if not most, literate communities. Where, then, can we find the important difference between the two types of cultures?

In the terminology of this inquiry, knowledge can be accumulated only at the expense of the *condensation* of certain boundaried spaces, since each finite human being can be aware of only a limited number of boundaried spaces from within a given perspectival framework at a given moment in time. At the same time there is no new knowledge that is not a *difference* with respect to prior knowledge. That is, as boundaried spaces are *condensed*, consciousness of each of those spaces and their meanings necessarily diminishes. At the same time, awareness of relationships between increasingly larger sets of *condensed* spaces (i.e., between what represents larger and larger wholes) demands increased abstraction in order that the *differences* may become apparent. This decreased consciousness of individual spaces as they are *condensed*, coupled with increasing levels of abstraction, leads to increasing possibility for committing error and inconsistency of thought. However, inconsistencies can be improved upon by means of a constant proliferation of countersign systems from increasingly broader critical perspectives. In this manner knowledge is always, as Peirce tells us, *self-corrective* (by way of *differences*).[3]

Now, given the finite perspectival framework and the memory limitations of each human being, the most effective storehouse for a growing multiplicity of *condensed* spaces and the increasingly broader critical perspectives is undoubtedly found in libraries: texts. The adequate library contains, far more than any given human and even more than all humans at a given point in time in a given civilization, a ready source of knowledge. Moreover, this knowledge, as marks-on-paper, readily calls for analysis, for critique, and for the generation of counterarguments in additional texts. Consequently, knowledge, when embodied in written texts, is most effectively *self-corrective*, since this knowledge exists as a static form of marks-on-paper, but, over time, it can be subjected to myriad interpretations within different contexts (see Merrell, 1981b, for further discussion of this topic). If there is no discernible line of demarcation between oral and literate cultures, it is nevertheless certain that the written sign allows for a relatively more rapid development of certain human cognitive capacities.

10.29 In sum, all countersign systems recorded in books or wherever are, like the exosomatic tools we create in order to work less, live better, go faster, and kill more effectively, part of our external world. They can be displayed, consumed, burned, abused, compared, and analyzed. They are also part of a perpetually dynamic and relatively open cultural system.

All living organisms create boundaried spaces, and all organisms construct and interpret the materialization of these boundaried spaces, on conscious and nonconscious levels and by learning or by inherited traits. However, few organisms construct *arbitrary sign systems* to serve as material manifestations of inner boundaried spaces. And only the human organism constructs, with such facility and by perpetually opening his sign systems, new conceptual frameworks at progressively higher levels of *organizational complexity*. The tendency toward open systems, however, is not without pitfalls, for the opposing tendency toward pathways of least resistance compels the human organism to *embed* itself deeper and deeper in nested systems of boundaried spaces to construct elaborate underlying knots (i.e., inconsistencies, paradoxes, binds). What follows in the next chapter is a description of what is perhaps part of the most excruciating knot into which we have tied ourselves.

Chapter 11

Concerning the Real Nature
of Texts

11.10 What Is a Reading?

11.11 A "thought experiment" in part derived from Bateson (1972, 279–337):

Imagine that I am chopping down a tree. I, imbued with my Cartesian mind/body view of things, assume that the tree is not part of myself, it is part of the objective world. The axe I use is an extension of myself, but beyond its practical use and beyond the fact that it is part of the set of things I possess, I consider it merely to be an object contiguous with other objects in the objective world.

However, my activity, in spite of what I believe it to be, is appropriately holistic; my tacit awareness remains on the totality of the act. The feel of the axe in my hand, the stability or instability of my stance, the difference between where I want the axe to fall and where it actually falls with each blow, the shape of the "V" in the trunk after each stroke: All these activities I regulate, considering that I am a relatively expert axeman, in a holistic, self-corrective way and almost "without thinking." I do not attempt to concentrate on each of my particular moves; that would be like a centipede trying to attend to each of its moves. The self-corrective process is mental, but it is brought about only within the context of the whole system: tree-eyes-brain-muscles-axe-stroke-tree, a system of constant feedback. The system is not in reality *me* against *tree*. It is a whole ensemble of *differences* rather than oppositions:

More correctly, we should spell the matter out as: (differences in tree)-(differences in retina)-(differences in brain)-(differences in muscles)-(differences in movement in axe)-(differences in tree), etc. What is transmitted around the circuit is transforms of differences (Bateson, 1972, 317–18).

Thus there is no all-or-nothing boundary between myself (my-*self*) and the tree. This is not to imply that I pretend in this brief inquiry to dispel the so-called mind/body problem. What I want to propose is not a question of saying what mind is but of proposing that mental states interact with the physical world by means of feedback channels. In this sense, finally to respond to the question, "What is consciousness consciousness of," it can only be stated that consciousness is consciousness of nothing outside its interaction, past or present, with the context of the physical world. It is an error, then, to talk of the interaction of two "substances": consciousness and the physical world, or mind and body. We must, in contrast, distinguish between two different forms of interacting states.

Yet when I complete my task I go home and tell my wife: "I cut down a tree." My language belies the real activity in which I was engaged. It makes absolute the distinction between my-*self* and a physical object. Does this mean that I am incarcerated within my language? Is there no other way to express in simple linguistic terms the real essence of my relationship with the physical object during my mental and physical activity?

11.12 In Greenlandic one does not say, "I kill it," or "I throw the stone," but "It dies to me," and "The stone is flying away from me." In other words, action is assimilated to impression. The perceiving being is integrated into the world and into the actions he perceives. This undoubtedly seems odd to us since our language assimilates perception to action. We see ourselves as acting upon a world "out there." With respect to our perceived action on trees, Waisman (1962, 108) tells us that:

> We say not only 'I cut the tree', but also 'I see the tree': the use of the same construction makes it appear as if the 'I' was the *subject* from which issued the seeing, and as if the seeing was a sort of action directed at the tree; nor are we any better off if we use the passive voice 'The tree is seen by me'—for now it looks as if something *happened* to the tree, as if it had to undergo or suffer my seeing it. Follow-

ing the clues of speech, we are led to interpret the world of experience one-sidedly, just as 'owing to the common philosophy of grammar', as Nietzsche put it, i.e., 'owing to the unconscious domination and guidance of similar grammatical functions' the way seems barred against certain other possibilities of world-interpretation.

Now, in light of tree-cutting, let us take another step by considering what we assume to be a different type of activity, the act of reading a text.

11.13 Exhausted after chopping down a tree, I sit down on the sofa to read a book. My eye moves along and rests for fleet moments on successive parts of a linear string of black marks-on-paper, rather than on one focal point as when chopping down the tree. Yet my activity is also holistic, the product of tacit awareness. I do not focus on each and every grapheme nor do I attend specifically to any of them. I try to understand the meaning behind the graphemes I perceive at a given moment, and to understand the relations between them and all other graphemes in each sentence, each page, and in the entire text. I can go back and reread, jot down notes to ponder over, make comparisons and contrasts. As I read I might frown, smile, chuckle, say "ah," "hm," etc. What does all this mean? It means precisely that I am trying in many ways to discover what I believe to be the focal point underlying the text, to discover meaning, to perceive humor, beauty, contradiction, ambiguity, error, truth, or whatever.

But this activity is not just mental. The shape and size of the letters and the texture of the book: Do they not have an effect on my reading? Where I am sitting, my surroundings, and whether or not I am comfortable have a bearing on my "feel" for the printed material before me. Also, my gestures, auditory expressions, my suspension of the reading to speculate on a problem are all part of this total activity. All this I do spontaneously and almost "without thinking," like my cutting down the tree. The conscious thoughts (boundaried spaces) that go through my mind during the act of reading have at least a partial manifestation in the physical world.

When I finish I tell my wife: "I read a book." The assertion seems to imply that my-*self* (my mind) has acted somehow on an aspect of the world in a way similar to my statement about cutting down a tree. However, is there not equally and in reality a series of *differences* involved in the act of reading? For instance: (differences in marks-on-paper)-(differences in retina)-(differences in brain)-(differences in gestures, in exclamations, in stops and starts, etc.)-(differences in eye movements along the page)-(differences in marks-on-paper), etc.

Why do we use physical metaphors for the act of reading, like, "I cracked the books," or "I hit the books"? Why must reading a text appear to be so physical? Why does our language not make a clear-cut distinction between reading a text and cutting a tree, or between cutting a tree and seeing a tree? If in our language the implied per-ceiver-actions-world relationships are fundamentally the same in, "I cut a tree," as in, "I see a tree," then is there any fundamental differ-ence between, "I cut a tree," and, "I read a book"? Or, if I say, "I demonstrated that I can exercise dominion over those trees," is it really any different from saying, "I proved that I can crack those books"? Does the subject-predicate and actor-action structure of our Western world languages "force" us to "see" the world in a particular way? Further discussion of the *differences* between tree-cutting and text-reading may offer us a clue.

11.14 On reading a text we project chiefly into a mental world, but only mediately through marks-on-paper. There is an interaction be-tween ourselves and that mental world that is manifested in the phys-ical world in no more than a few vague and indirect ways. We receive information indirectly from the marks-on-paper that does not imme-diately and necessarily lead to action on the physical world, although it can greatly affect our mental world. Hence, nothing physical or causal that is of an empirically definable nature necessarily occurs in the act of reading. On the other hand, cutting down a tree with the mind acting as a helmsman, there is a definite physical cause-and-effect system that can ideally be measured. We project into the world and very visibly interact with it in a physical sense. We receive infor-mation from a focal point along the trunk of the tree, like an animal receiving information from its environment, and this serves to alter our movements. After the task is completed we might say: "I caused the tree to fall," or, "I forced the tree down." In contrast, we would not ordinarily say: "I caused the book to be read," or, "I forced a reading of the book." Nevertheless, the simplified statement, "I read a book," implies a subject/object or mind/body universe just as does the complementary statement, "I cut down a tree."

We can say: "I forced the nut off this rusty bolt," "I forced the painted-shut window open," "I forced the drunk out of the bar." But can we "force" a person to read a book; that is, can we really and properly "force" him to read a book with a sincere desire to satisfy his curiosity with respect to the messages that lie within it? Or can we "force" a person to believe in God—that is, outside brainwashing him? Or can we force him to be spontaneous, to doubt, to be skeptical? We can drive a nail or a car. But can we, in the same physical sense, "drive" a person crazy or "drive" him to drink? Yet this is the way we speak. It would in essence not be overly absurd, given our embedded view of the relationship between the *self* and the world, to say that we "forced" a book to be read, or that we "caused" the marks on the page to "jump up" and "strike" our retinas. However, it is merely one more step in the same direction. It can be stated that to "force" or "cause" another person to read a book or to "force" oneself to read a book is in essence to "force" or "cause" that book to be read, since that person and the book are equally part of the objective world and separate from the "forcing" and "causing" self. To state that one "forced a book to be read," then, is simply to omit the reader from the utterance. This is similar to Waisman's above example of the passive voice.

The metaphors to which I have been referring illustrate our propensity for causalist-mechanistic-energetic patterns of speech with respect to interactions between mind and world. This is of course part of our Cartesian Western world epistemology. Let us now observe one of the implications of this view of the universe and of ourselves.

11.15 During the process of reading, the eye explores marks-on-paper and acts upon them. However, this action is more complex than acting on a tree with an axe. Reading entails, in light of sections 7.31-7.34, a willing or unwilling suspension or unsuspension of belief or disbelief, and a constant oscillation between the two complementary alternatives presented by the paradoxical injunction between self and text. That is, between the self and a mental world mediated by the text. The relationship between the self and this mental world may be conceived in the Cartesian sense as that of opposition and identity. That is, as a countertext, the text exists in simple opposition to other texts, and in the sense that it is part of the physical world, it is opposed to the self-mind. Yet for the reader to willingly suspend disbelief in the act of reading he must identify himself with the text. The text is therefore ordinarily considered to be written and read in terms of a symmetrical and contradictory relationship of opposition/identity.

However, in reality this either-or "digitalization," illustrated by the "inside-outside" of the oscillatory model, is complemented and mediated by the mind's capacity to perceive continuity through time such that neither opposition nor identity seem to exist but both opposition and identity coexist in "simultaneity." This coexistence can constitute the larger holistic frame of which self and mental world, text and texts, are all a part. To be either "inside" or "outside" the text would be to comprehend it only at the symmetrical level of opposition and identity. In contrast, when one is neither "inside" nor "outside" but tacitly and consciously aware of both "inside" and "outside," one is potentially capable of conceiving and perceiving things from the larger frame in terms of *comparative differences* rather than of mere categorical opposition and identity.

This potential remains chiefly beyond the capacity of the lower organisms, for example the flatworm from the series of "thought experiments" in Chapter 1. Its choices, as well as its perceptual capabilities, can be none other than either-or. It is, speaking in the sense of Popper, a "dogmatist." On the other hand, the human organism can, by comparison and contrast, relatively easily exercise critical faculties within the argumentative mode—though, of course, there always exists the natural tendency to become a "dogmatist" also, for it offers a world of greater security. To put this another way, the animal organism is part of its world, for it is incapable, in the human sense at least, of consciously setting itself apart from its world. The human has, by conscious cogitation and then by generations of more deeply embedded thought and language use, artificially brought about the subject/object and mind/body split, yet he is potentially capable, at the mind level, and at metalevels of consciousness, of reintegrating himself with his world—and with his interrelated world of texts. In fact, all human beings, to a degree and whether they know it or not, exercise such a reintegration when perceiving their world or when putting themselves *into* texts. The "oscillation model" gives ample testimony to this phenomenon.

11.20 The Potentially Infinite Nature of Texts, Readings, and Countertexts

11.21 Language use from within the Cartesian-Newtonian causalist-mechanistic-energetic world view implies a reductionism directed toward some definite end, such as "cutting down a tree" or "reading a book." The completed task is presumed to be an accomplished fact.

It is presumed that there will ordinarily be no further interaction between subject and tree trunk or between subject and marks-on-paper. The end product of both activities is equivalent to the absolute and determinate effect of a cause. That is, the subject is now in a new state of readiness for the next event.

The real problem here is that, as ecological studies have demonstrated, man's action on nature is not unidirectional. There exists an exceedingly intricate system of ongoing feedback channels from nature to man and from man to nature. The cutting down of a tree is not an absolute once-and-for-all fact. The tree's existence was intelligible only within the context of an intricate set of interconnected interactions between it and its environment, and the fallen tree must therefore bring about some degree of change in that entire environment and hence in the totality of man's environment, no matter how minute that change may be in this particular case. Moreover, the mind, having interacted via the body with the physical environment, is also irreversibly changed as a result of the action. However, after chopping down a tree the subsequent statement, "I can cut down a tree," falsely reinforces the cutter's concept of dominion over his environment. It provides part of a general guide to future action within the framework of the causalist-mechanistic-energetic world view implied by the use of that statement.

11.22 The act of reading also involves feedback channels. The reading of a book acts upon the reader in such a way that one cannot simply say, "I read a book," as if it were an absolute and accomplished fact. Reading a book, like chopping down a tree, should not be looked upon as final and determinate. True, after perceiving the last mark-on-paper the interaction between reader and a particular physical object in the world ceases. But texts do not correspond directly to the physical world. They are mediated by "mental" worlds and hence they act upon the "mental" world(s) of the reader while the reader acts upon the "mental" world to which the text refers. Such action is an ongoing process, for THE HUMAN ORGANISM POSSESSES MEMORY.

How does this process occur? Assume that the reader never returns to a particular text he just finished reading. It can be stated that he cannot analyze the text in terms of its visual graphemic aspect. He cannot critically probe the text, comparing and contrasting statements within the text and comparing and contrasting the text with other texts. Yet his "reading" has become an irreversible part of his "mental" world(s). And, it is now an amorphous, constantly changing thing that is progressively being embedded in those "mental" world(s), although he may not be aware of the fact. He may believe that he still "knows" the text. However, it may have become for him *embedded* or "mythified," as do oral texts in nonliterate cultures. Indeed, his conception of the text will now be restricted to the same memory limitations as all nonliterate discourse. Consequently, there will be superficial change without his awareness of that change.

An example. A man reads Marx, believes what he reads, and becomes a Marxist. Ten years later, without having reread Marx and having read only a few contemporary interpretations and vulgarizations of Marxist thought, he now holds opinions that have become surprisingly un-Marxian even though he believes himself to be an orthodox adherent to the philosophy. The same could occur to a newly converted Christian, Freudian, new leftist, "hippie," or what have you.

Hence the notion put forth above becomes evident. That boundaried spaces are dynamic in spite of the relatively static characteristic of their names. The next step is to specify an epistemology capable of accounting for this important phenomenon.

11.23 In contrast to the epistemology of the causalist-mechanistic-energetic world view that presupposes static and determinate readings of texts, I submit the following proposition that logically follows from the four initial AXIOMS and from PROPOSITIONS I through V:

PROPOSITION VI: *Countersigns-examples-arguments-texts within human societies constitute a continual interaction between a potentially infinite array over time of interconnected theories, concepts, ideas, intuitions, emotions, visions, fictions, etc.*

The causalist-mechanistic-energetic view is like Newtonian laws of motion with action between two or more isolated bodies. PROPOSITION VI, in contrast, allows for only a *relative* autonomy of sets of domains that are interconnected by increasingly complex feedback channels. The former view is determinate; the latter implies an ongoing process, for it remains inside mental worlds, without direct external referents in the physical world; therefore it implies the potential existence over time of an infinite number of possibilities.

I believe PROPOSITION VI is preferable. The potential infinity of mental worlds is incompatible with an epistemology of individualism implied by the ordinary image of "chopping down a tree" or "reading a book." However, PROPOSITION VI can only be realized—albeit incompletely, since total realization implies infinity—through the continual subjection of texts to critical probing in order to reveal new problem situations and new contradictions, in order to perpetually generate countertexts. Only through the continuous appearance of texts and countertexts can the potential infinity of mental worlds be tapped effectively, not by individuals, but by the collectivity of human minds. And this process can occur most effectively in literate cultures, and only among minds incessantly probing, testing, and analyzing written texts.

11.24 No really well-founded conclusions can be forthcoming from an epistemology based on the finitude of possible theories, concepts, ideas, intuitions, emotions, visions, fictions, etc., in texts. Such an epistemology presupposes that knowledge as portrayed through texts is directed toward the ideal of some static and absolute Truth, which itself requires infinity for its conception. That is, it presupposes that given human finitude, Truth is inaccessible by ordinary means, yet it can be known by the transcendental mind, by the spirit, or whatever. The problem is that such conception entails, once again, the subject/object and mind/body split, but what is more serious, it inconsistently merges finity into infinity. In contrast, since, according to the hypothesis propounded here, there can be no end to the possible range of mental worlds and text interrelatedness, there can also be no end to the probing, testing, and criticism of texts and the generation of countertexts.

This hypothesis of infinite potentiality is necessary, for every relatively sophisticated and complex text that can possibly be formulated invariably contains some error, problem, contradiction, omission, inadequacy. This is simply because each text is necessarily capable of accounting for only an exceedingly small aspect of the world or of mental worlds. No text can be complete, and if there are pretentions of completeness there inevitably exists inconsistency and contradiction.[1] In this sense, a reading of all texts, past, present, and future, cannot possibly lead to any form of knowledge that is complete, completable, or completely free of problem situations. On the contrary, such a reading would lead to an unending process in which knowledge would be either increasing or decreasing, but it could never be static; therefore it could never be complete. The process of knowledge acquisition suggested here is derived from interacting and interconnected sign systems capable of encompassing broader and broader domains, of constantly revealing new problem situations and inconsistencies. As these domains continue to be opened to new knowledge, Absolute Truth (i.e., in the sense of causalist-mechanistic-energetic epistemology), that ideal world of perfect order, continues to recede beyond new horizons. The quest is, fortunately for us, unending (see, for example, Bohm, 1957; also Grene, 1974, and Popper, 1974).

11.30 Why the Primacy of Abstractions?

11.31 Let us recapitulate by returning to the human being as an abstracting organism. The notion of the potential infinity of texts, countertexts, and mental worlds leads us to regard each text as, given human fallibility and human finitude, not more than an incomplete abstraction. It is inexorably a *condensation*, which implies some *expanded* form of tacit or nonconscious awareness. Of course, we must utilize our abstractions, for it is impossible to incorporate the totality of even the most minute aspect of the world or of a mental world into a single text. We are, each one of us, inextricably condemned to abstract. Nevertheless, as Whitehead tells us, although we must abstract, we can certainly maintain a state of reserved suspicion *vis-à-vis* our abstractions. Such suspicion leads eventually to an opening of texts and of mental worlds to inquiry. Countertexts inevitably follow.

According to the assertions in the above sections, nothing has been written down in the form of a text that is capable of being eternally defined in an absolute and invariant way. Every sign, every statement, every text, however fundamental it may be, always changes, with successive readings and under different circumstances, to become something other than what it was or could otherwise have been. In light of the oscillatory nature of sign and text perception, with each transition from "inside" to "outside" there has been a time differential, and accompanying this time differential is a degree of change in space, no matter how small. After each successive oscillation a sign (or text) never remains identical with itself, it is never exactly what it previously was. I repeat: You can never step in the same river twice. What is the ultimate consequence of this notion?

11.32 There exists a potentially infinite stream of texts (cf. PROPO-

SITIONS I and VI). Each of these texts, as no more than an exceedingly rough abstraction, should ideally be explained in terms of what it does not say rather than by what it says—but, then, to say what a text does not say would require an infinite text; hence the task would be impossible. On the other hand, to attend to a text solely with respect to its quality as an abstraction, in isolation from all other texts, would be as if we could reduce ourselves to microscopic dimensions, enter the proverbial river, and with a protractor measure the angle of the hydrogen atoms with respect to the oxygen atoms in each water molecule. In the process we would not be aware that we were supposed to be getting "wet." That is, we could not "fill in the gaps" in order to possess awareness of the macroscopic qualities of the river.

When reading a text what we actually do is submerge ourselves in it, and in so doing, we perceive continuity by filling in the gaps left by the necessary abstractive process of writing (cf. PROPOSITION II). In certain respects we accomplish our task so well that we are not even aware that the gaps exist. This is for two reasons.

First, at the microlevel we are biologically endowed with the capacity to fill in the spaces by means of the paradoxical "inside" and "outside" oscillatory process. Second, at the macrolevel we conceive/perceive texts from within a partly culture-bound and partly idiosyncratic conceptual framework consisting of an increasingly complex Chinese box of embedded spaces (cf. PROPOSITION V). Boundaries between these spaces have been conveniently "erased" such that we tend to believe we "see" a continuum. There are for us ordinarily no gaps, for we simply and categorically believe that this is the way things are. We are therefore by and large unaware of many of the category mistakes, contradictions, and paradoxes created by these embedded spaces. Consequently, we may tie ourselves into conceptual knots without knowing precisely what the problem is. Only by a progressive de-embedment of the text's boundaried spaces may we be able to recognize the gaps and become aware of discontinuities (cf. PROPOSITION II), in order to conceive/perceive new continuities (cf. PROPOSITIONS III and IV). This implies concomitant awareness of at least part of what remains unsaid in the text that otherwise might have been said. And, as outlined in 10.23, this awareness of textual *differences* through sameness and similarity presupposes the ability to be skeptical, to doubt, to disbelieve, etc.[2]

11.33 What I am saying applies equally well to the text the reader now has before him. It applies to all texts about texts, and to theories *of* texts. Since texts interact at increasingly complex levels with all other texts within their contexts, given time, these contexts will also suffer change. Hence, any well-formulated and unvarying theory of texts must eventually be opened to change. Any given theory can be applicable only for a period of time short enough that no appreciable changes occur in the basic semiotic properties of the data to which the theory applies. No theory can be Absolute, permanent, or exhaustive. The choice of a particular theory, therefore, is dependent on what appears to be the most suitable explication of the data at a given point in time (see Bohm, 1957).

11.34 The advantage of the hypothesis of the potential infinity of texts and mental worlds is that what during a particular time appear to be irresolvable contradictions and problem situations present, over time, no real barrier. With potentially infinitely changing ideas, concepts, theories, intuitions, emotions, visions, fictions, etc., and their corresponding texts and mental worlds, each and every contradiction and problem situation that pops up can eventually be resolved. Nothing can be absolutely unknowable through time and nothing can be absolutely known at any given moment in time. Rather than wallow in the muck of a relativistic epistemology that can only culminate in nihilism, this hypothesis allows us to maintain the idea that any particular system and any particular theory constitutes only an approximation, only a relative truth, along with the optimistic vision of there perpetually existing the possibility of discovering-inventing newer and more broadly based portions of truth *ad infinitum*.

Epilogue: Steps Beyond

Call this book a set of spaces: $\bigcirc_1$, $\bigcirc_2$, $\bigcirc_3$, ... $\bigcirc_n$. You may have crossed each and every one of these spaces. But you have also recrossed (embedded) many of them (AXIOM III).

Name the spaces thus: $a, b, c, \ldots n$. Many of these names have been negated (forgotten) as their corresponding spaces were recrossed (embedded) (AXIOM IV).

Call these recrossed (embedded) spaces and negated (canceled) names *gaps*. You can fill in part of the *gaps* by rereading the book (AXIOMS I and III).

Many *gaps* inevitably remain, but you can and do (tacitly) fill in some of them with spaces you yourself constructed in order to perceive a continuum (PROPOSITIONS II, III, and IV).

Your-*self*, that is, your conscious and nonconscious *self*, is in this act interjected into the self-constructed spaces. Your-*self* has become part of these spaces. These spaces have become part of your-*self*.

In time, as more and more of these spaces are recrossed (embedded) and more and more names are negated (forgotten), *condensation* of spaces occurs along with concomitant *expansion* of your tacit awareness of the content of the book: perpetual embedment (PROPOSITION V).

On the other hand, your-*self* and the book gradually tend to become one over time. The book becomes one with all books. Your-*self* becomes one with all *selfs:* perpetual de-embedment (PROPOSITIONS I and VI).

However, your-*self*, the book, all books, can never be static. The river continues. An interesting tale it could tell, but that, of course, would be an unending story.

NOTES

Preface

1. See Merrell (1980c) for a more specific inquiry into the structure of all written texts. The present study is a companion volume to another work (Merrell, 1980b), which discusses the nature of fictions at an equally broad level.

2. The approach taken here is commensurate with Sebeok's (1977) holistic "ecumenical" vision wherein, as Peirce maintained, not only is there a continuum between the natural and the cultural realms of signs, but man, in addition to processing signs, is himself a sign.

3. In the following chapters I generally bracket out the heated Chomskyan debate over whether language is species-specific. I am not interested in syntactic structures or the grammar rules of natural languages per se, but in the general semiotic foundations of all communicative systems and in the specific semiotic foundations of natural languages insofar as they are used to construct and perceive written texts. The focus of my inquiry is how general perspectives of the world, habits of thought, and conceptual frameworks change by means of the language of written texts. Ultimately I attempt to formulate a "logic" capable of accounting for the general capacity for abstraction that lies at the heart of all structured written texts.

I am not interested in the functional characteristics of human languages or any "design features" that might set natural human languages apart from animal languages (for examples of such studies see Bronowski, 1967; Hewes, 1971; Hockett, 1959). I assume that there are obvious differences between animal and human languages, both in degree and in kind. But there are also obvious similarities. If I appear to favor certain similarities it is because I attempt to begin at the beginning, at the point where, at least in human beings, cognitive faculties and linguistic faculties converge. If it also appears that I am anthropomorphizing animal forms of communication it is only for the sake of illustration and brevity. There is no attempt to impute a human form of intentionality in animal behavior or to specify any level of humanlike consciousness in the animal; resolution of that problem, if indeed a resolution is possible, pertains to specialists in linguistics and ethology.

4. The most prominent of these scholars are N.R. Hanson (1958), Toulmin (1953), Polanyi (1958), Kuhn (1970), and Feyerabend (1975).

5. Of course, Derrida sets his own "grammatology" apart from French "semiology." However, "semiotics," defined in the broad Peircean sense, would, I believe, incorporate the Derridean notion of the grapheme (for a detailed discussion, see Merrell, 1981b).

Introduction

1. Crick points out that according to the positivistic, ethnocentric approach, the world must be one way, OUR way. For instance, alchemy is usually studied as an erroneous and misguided science. But this is fallacious, for alchemy developed an elaborate system by means of metaphors, which is "no less coherent than those we call scientific" (Crick, 1976, 148;

see also Jarvie and Agassi, 1967, 1973). In this light, and with respect to the present inquiry, it is appropriate to assume that there is an underlying commonality between all written texts, whether scientific or mythical, mathematical or poetic. At the deepest level they all manifest, intentionally or unintentionally on the part of their author, an elaborate system of thought.

2. From various perspectives see, in anthropology, Douglas (1966, 1973), Horton (1967), Lee (1959), Needham (1973); in psychology, Rosch (1974, 1978); in philosophy, Cassirer (1953); and in epistemology, Bloor (1976), Feyerabend (1975), N. R. Hanson (1958), and Polanyi (1958).

3. For illustration of how this general approach is developed in varied ways and from within diverse disciplines, see Arnheim (1969), Berger and Luckmann (1966), Bruner (1957), Gombrich (1960), Neisser (1967), Paivio (1971), Piaget (1973), and Popper (1972).

4. F. A. Hanson (1979) charts a middle course between what he calls "objectivism" (truth as correspondence with the facts) and "relativism" (truth as conformity with the standards of the tradition). He calls his alternative "contextualism," which, "like relativism, allows that truth and knowledge may vary from one culture or mode of discourse to another, but which like objectivism, maintains the notion that all people inhabit a single world that exists in determinate form and independently of what people say or think about it" (F. A. Hanson, 1979, 517). Though I would tend to be less of a "realist" than Hanson (see Merrell, 1980b, 1981b), I believe this approach effectively breaches a long-standing dichotomy. For my part, I would tend to place our propensity to select at the biological level, where all humans share certain common assumptions about their world, and at the linguistic-cultural-private level, which varies from one context to another.

5. See Goody (1977), from whom I have drawn this triad. I must here also acknowledge my debt to Derrida (especially 1967), whose criticism of Western world "logocentrism," particularly since the advent of Saussurian linguistics, and whose call for a "grammatology" is now well-known. Though I have reservations concerning the value of some of Derrida's assertions (see Merrell, 1981b), this inquiry will in general place emphasis on "writing." Nevertheless, as I will argue below, there is no all-or-nothing opposition between oral and literate traditions.

6. I am putting forth the notion, now rather common, that all normal humans possess fundamentally the same biological capacity, but that this capacity undergoes specific development within various cultural milieus. This capacity can be unfolded differently between members of literate and oral communities. And such unfolding can be largely dependent on the language one speaks. However, that language determines perception and even world views, and that it alone accounts for the distinction from one culture to another remains an intriguing, and at this time only partly answered, question. One of the most interesting studies along this line is that of Lee, (1959) who, following Whorf's work, demonstrates how the relatively "non-lineal" mode of thought of the Trobrianders is manifest even in their speech patterns—which are their most patently "lineal" form of communication. This "lineal" versus "non-lineal" thought brings up the complementarity between left-right hemisphere cerebral processes, each hemisphere with its specialization, but constantly interacting with the other (see Sperry, 1969, 1970; Gazzinaga, 1970; Bogen, 1969; Bogen and Bogen, 1969).

It has been speculated, following neurophysiological studies, that there are connections between the lateralization of cerebral processes and cross-cultural differences (Ten Houton and Kaplan, 1973; Paredes and Hepburn, 1976). If such is indeed the case, then it is reasonable to suppose that what Hall (1976) calls "high-context" cultures would be less "lineal," whereas "low-context" (Western) cultures would be more "lineal" and hence more explicitly verbal, with less emphasis on kinetic communication. Fernandez (1980), while studying an oral, and we would presume a relatively "non-lineal" culture, discovered that the riddles he gave his subjects were not properly understood by them. Western riddles are usually context-free; in contrast, the subjects persisted in looking for meaning within some broad, holistic context. Moreover, with respect to Western cultures, the studies of Bernstein (1975) and Labov (1972) demonstrate that, respectively, working-class English children and culturally marginalized minority groups also tend to develop their own relatively "non-lineal" context-dependent and nonverbal forms of communication that depart from traditional norms.

I have here cited only a few examples. Though empirical evidence for left-right hemisphere complementarity is mounting, it is not within the scope of this study to treat this topic in detail.

7. I must confess at this point that I am not comfortable with this "oral culture"/"literate culture" distinction. The so-called "literate cultures" are not non-oral, nor are "oral cultures" necessarily less sophisticated due to their lack of writing. Yet, focusing on written texts as I will during this inquiry, I believe some distinction must be made.

1. Steps toward a Foundation of Boundaried Spaces

1. This notion of a boundaried space is comparable to, and indeed it is drawn from, Spencer-Brown's (1969) "mark of distinction" and from Peirce's "cuts," which are fundamental to his "existential graphs" (see Roberts, 1973; also the use of "cuts" in Merrell, 1980b). The act of marking off a single boundaried space from the unboundaried makes possible the coming of consciousness of that boundaried space, somewhat like Peirce's "Firstness," the raw, present, immediate, and spontaneous sensation. Such a sensation, or boundaried space, totally unrelated to any other sensations, is at this point a "*sleeping* consciousness. . . . a potential consciousness" (Peirce, 1960, 6.221). It cannot be part of articulate thought, for if it is asserted, "it has lost its characteristic innocence; for assertion always implies a denial of something else. Stop to think of it, and it has flown!" (Peirce, 1960, 1.357). In this sense, each boundaried space, like each primitive sensation, is in itself what it is for itself, with no reference to anything else.

2. A somewhat implicit objective in this inquiry is to reveal the evolution of form, from primitive beginnings to the written sign to the text. This evolution entails a transition from the undifferentiated to the differentiated, from homogeneity to heterogeneity. In Peirce's (1960, 6.196) words, the becoming of form "begins or, at any rate, has for an early stage of it, a vague [and infinite] potentiality; and that either is or is followed by a continuum of forms having a multitude of dimensions too great for the individual dimensions to be distinct. It must be by a contraction of the vagueness of that potentiality of everything in general, but of nothing in particular, that the world of forms comes about."

3. Contrary to what might appear to be the case, I do not here fall into

the trap of induction. While it might be safely asserted that a "space" repeatedly marked off by a computer is in a way identical, it is not in the same sense for an organism, animal or human. The fundamental doctrine underlying the notion of induction is that of the primacy of repetitions, whether logical or psychological (in the Humean sense). In contrast to this doctrine, Popper (1959, 420–22) rightly points out that the repetition B of an event A does not give an event identical to A. All repetitions are no more than approximate, and their similarity is no more than relative, for they can be similar in different respects (see also Goodman, 1972, 437-47). On the other hand, perception of similarity or identity always presupposes, a priori, a point of view. A similarity might exist in one respect within one context, and in another within another. Yet the fact remains that we do perceive (or believe we perceive) similarity, and even identity, for otherwise we would be incapable of generating universals. Hence the two spaces in question here can be "potentially" given the same value—that is, the space can be "potentially" perceived as a universal.

4. I cannot overestimate the influence of Spencer-Brown's *Laws of Form* on this book. *Laws of Form* not only reveals the elegant arithmetic form constituting the basis of Boolean algebra, but, of interest to all who contemplate the mysteries of human existence, it provides insight into, as will be demonstrated below, the possible roots of consciousness and of the consciousness of time. Written by a mathematician, engineer, poet, psychiatrist, chess master, accomplished glider pilot, and sports correspondent, it is truly the work of a genius.

5. Since I will use the analog/digital distinction below, a summary definition of the terms is necessary here. A mercury thermometer without graduations is an elementary example of an "analog" system. Temperature increase or decrease is described along a more-or-less continuum. A graduated thermometer, in contrast, is "digitalized" into increments for more precise readings. A slide rule also operates along a sliding more-or-less scale that is graduated into "digital bits"; hence it operates both on "analog" and "digital" properties. The entire scale of a slide rule or a graduated thermometer can be viewed in a holistic (analog) and general way, but a particular "bit" (digit) of information cannot be read with precision; it can only be a nearer or further approximation. On the other hand, a pocket calculator is more strictly a "digital" machine that shows a specific answer with precision, but the entire system is, unlike that of the slide rule or the graduated thermometer, unavailable to view at a given instant; only a small number of "bits" may be read.

Hence, "analog" systems are continuous throughout; "digital" systems are discontinuous. "Analog" systems are ordinarily processed and perceived holistically as a presence of or an absence of; "digital" systems are generated from constituent units or "bits" of information into messages that can then be broken up ("analyzed") and perceived as isolated parts. (For more details on my use of these terms see Bateson, 1972; Goodman, 1976; von Neumann, 1958; Sebeok, 1972; Wilden, 1972).

6. The name (Symbol or Logosign in the Peircean sense) entails a level of abstraction higher than that of the boundaried space or consciousness of it as opposed to other boundaried spaces. Naming presupposes a connection between something (an object) and someone (an interpreter), and so it is a medium (Peirce, 1960, 1.297).

7. At this point I am not heeding Derrida's (1967) critique of the Saus-

surean indissoluble connection between signifier (the expression) and signified (the content). What is being considered here is, at a more primitive level of perception, what the sign is ordinarily taken to be: an expression that is simultaneously its content, and an entity that somehow, like "word magic," embodies the thing to which it refers (such as Pavlov's "neurotic" dog). At a later stage in this inquiry we will observe the fallacy inherent in this Saussurean concept.

8. This sameness should be interpreted like the repeated spaces (see note 3).

9. Hence there is no end to the number of spaces and names that can potentially be used to represent the world. That is, there is no end to the number of possible languages and to the number of possible cultural perspectives. This topic will be discussed in later sections.

10. Significantly, Peirce's "Firstness," like the boundaried space, is a potential that can become an actual item of conscious experience. That item of experience, "Secondness," presupposes the idea of *not*, or *other*, from which a concept of "reality" can then be constructed (Peirce, 1960, 1.324-25).

11. What follows from this point onward, as will be seen, is tense, modal markers, syntax; that is, language. Consequently "analog" icons (boundaried spaces) become manifested in "digital" word strings (sentences). However, such complexity is beyond the concerns of the present sections.

12. It bears mentioning that this species-specificity is not synonymous with "language competence" in the sense of Chomsky. The potential for unlimited semiotic variability I speak of is more primitive than the language generating component. It is a more general semiotic component including the language component as a subset, which Chomsky vaguely refers to in *Reflections on Language* (1972) (see also Merrell, 1980c).

2. The Invention of Our Mental Worlds

1. This formulation is akin to Meinong's theory of "mental objects" (see especially Findlay, 1963; Howell, 1979; Parsons, 1975; Routley, 1979; Smith, 1975; also, Merrell, 1980b). Meinong claims that all mental states are directed toward something and thus they possess distinguishing features. In this sense what is not is as important as what is. According to this notion, knowledge not only pertains to existents, that is, to the empirical objects of science and metaphysics; knowledge also pertains to the arts, imagination, and all inner experiences. How else, a Meinongian would ask, could theories of the "real world" have come about except by virtue of imaginary worlds (i.e., Pythagoras' spheres, phlogiston, the aether, Einstein's relativity, "deviant" logics, transfinite numbers, Hilbert's space of infinite dimensions, Dada art, recent developments in quantum mechanics, etc.)? We must conclude that objects that do not, and perhaps cannot, exist are nonetheless genuine objects and parts of the total experienced world.

This implies first, that there are objects that do not exist, and second, that nonexistent objects can nonetheless be spoken of in such a way that they can be made the subject of a predication that is conceived as if it were true, hence they are constituted in some way or other. Therefore, there are existent and nonexistent objects, just as there are possible and impossible objects. The "real world" is that of the range of existent objects, while a "gold mountain" is nonexistent but conceivably a possible object in a possible world, and a "square circle" is a nonexistent and impossible object. Nevertheless, nonexistent objects are as real—mentally, that is—as existent objects, the only difference is that they do not exist!

2. Hereafter the term our/the/a "real world," when in quotation marks, will denote the physical world as seen from a particular perspective, and from within a particular conceptual framework and world view. Since, as was posited in 1.37, human beings, given past, present, and future times and places, possess the potentiality for an unlimited number of variations in the sets of boundaried spaces they can generate, their number of "real worlds" must be equally unlimited.

3. Consider, for example, the "wave-particle" duality of matter according to contemporary physics. While "waves" and "particles" are imaginable, they are not so in simultaneity—in contrast to the juxtaposition of a "horn" and a "horse" to form a "unicorn"—for they are mutually contradictory. Yet matter paradoxically manifests, depending on the particular conditions, the characteristics both of "waves" and "particles."

4. See, in general, Bronowski (1978), Bruner (1962), Hadamard (1945), Koestler (1945), Wechsler (1978); also, for further discussion, see Merrell (1980b).

5. It should be mentioned that my emphasis on visual perception represents no attempt to de-emphasize other forms of perception. However, since I will be considering the perception of graphemic signs on paper representing words (and other symbols) in the written text, my concern understandably lies predominantly in the area of our perception of visual data.

6. For example, in sociology see Berger and Luckmann (1967); in psychology, Laing (1967) and Lilly (1967, 1977); in philosophy, Melhuish (1973); in science, Kuhn (1970) and Feyerabend (1975); and in art, Gombrich (1960).

7. The term "proposition" is used in the mathematical sense of a statement that has been or is to be demonstrated and that is capable of being believed, doubted, or denied by a subsequent counterproposal and counterargument.

8. Quarks are elusive symmetrical patterns of elementary particles that have thus far escaped empirical verification. Their existence is postulated in an attempt to bring some semblance of order to an otherwise chaotic collection of subnuclear particles. However, if the nuclear physicists try long and hard enough to empirically verify the existence of quarks, perhaps, as has been the case of other scientific theories of the past, it may in the future be unquestionably assumed that they exist. Ultimately, as relativity physics, quantum mechanics, and even Eastern mystical philosophy suggest, structures and phenomena, things and events, are creations of man's categorizing mind. In the beginning is the word that differentiates. Words beget other words, and those beget other words, and so on ad infinitum. Quarks and all other categories of thought (i.e., mesons, aether, phlogiston, Rousseauian man, the classless society, etc.) have been created-invented as a result of man's asking questions of nature and of the nature of himself, of seeking information in nature and in himself, and of sending information to nature and to himself. Most of the categories of thought that have been so derived have become a part of our "real" and even of our perceived world.

9. This topic will be taken up later. For the present, this Möbius strip

illustration is necessary in order to establish my propositions for the semiotic foundations of human perception and conception. For a compatible discussion of this topic, see Fernandez (1974), who, though without allusion to the Möbius strip, demonstrates that metaphor creation entails "analog" linkage between what would otherwise be construed as discontinuous "digital" entities.

10. For discussion of topological "catastrophes," see Thom (1975), Zeeman (1976), and Woodcock and Davis (1978). See also Sebeok (1976a) for comments on the potential usefulness of "catastrophe theory" to semiotics. Also, Merrell (1980c) for possible applications to text analysis.

3. Steps toward the Mediation of Contradictory Spaces

1. It must be pointed out that such metalevels, accessible to human consciousness, are necessary before the possibility of speaking about aggressive activity, and hence before the existence of ethical or moral standards of conduct, or before talk about ethics or morals can exist. Such studies as those of Ardrey (1967), Lorenz (1966), and Morris (1967) afford the extremely pessimistic view that humans, like animals, can exercise little to no control over their biological compulsions (see also Callan, 1970). On the contrary, I believe we can overcome many or most of these limitations if we really think about them for awhile.

2. I will not review in detail nor will I take up the standing debate over whether or not primates have learned to "speak" a human language. For a discussion in favor of the apes see Fouts and Rigby (1977), Gardner and Gardner (1969), Hewes (1973), Linden (1976), Premack (1970, 1971), and Rumbaugh (1977). For the alternative view see Bronowski (1967), Bronowski and Bellugi (1970), R. Brown (1970), Chomsky (1968), Lenneberg (1967), and Pribram (1971). On the other hand, Sebeok (1979, Chapters 3, 4, and 5) has recently pointed out that the ape trainers often convey subtle cues to their subjects, like the "Clever Hans" phenomenon, which allow them to respond in accord with their trainer's expectations. If such is indeed the case, then the apes' metaphor-metonymical activity I allude to is not of their own doing. Nonetheless, whether authored by human or animal, the mechanism by means of which this activity is generated is the same, and hence the examples retain their validity.

3. The hierarchy from (a) to (i) is, of course, simple and fundamental in principle. This does not necessarily discount its value. It is interesting to note that, without going into detail here, the set of relations in the hierarchy can be reformulated into what in cybernetics are called "logical nets" (which were conceived as a possible model of the neural network in the brain and which follow the Boolean principles of negation, addition, and multiplication) (see Klir and Valach, 1967). This observation leads to the rather speculative assumption that the primitive roots of the global-macroscopic level of semiotic systems might manifest certain properties in common with the local-microscopic level of neural activity in the communicating organism. This is not to imply that all "mental events" are nothing but "brain events." That is, what I am saying, at least with respect to the human mind and to human communicational systems, is not "reductionistic," nor am I a "physicalist" in the ordinary sense. I do not argue that all

"mental events" formulated from within a semiotic system can and will some day be reformulated as "physical events" in the brain. Neither am I a "mentalist" in the Cartesian sense. I believe that at least theoretically it is possible to account for "mental events" in terms of "physical events" in the brain, though it is certainly not possible in practice (cf. the work of Mc-Culloch and Pitts, von Neumann, Turing, and others; see discussion in Singh, 1966; and above all, see Hofstadter, 1979).

The preceding statements might appear to be mutually contradictory. This is not actually the case since they rest on distinct levels. What is a theoretical possibility can remain so indefinitely, without ever being absolutely empirically demonstrated. The problem is rather similar to the infinity paradox rather than to a simple contradiction. The mind that discovers how to specify all "mental events" as "physical events," or the mind that discovers how to construct and constructs a machine model of itself, is at that point no longer the same mind. It will have expanded (evolved), like the receding outer reaches of the universe, to a new metalevel that cannot be empirically demonstrated by previous discoveries and models. In other words, if the mind were capable of looking at itself in a mirror to see how it worked, it would only see itself as it was before the necessary information, traveling at the speed of light, progressed from the mind to the mirror and back again. The mind can never see itself as it is.

Consequently, the best we can do with any theory of mind, or of the semiotic foundations of any communicational system, is describe how new boundaried spaces and perspectives are conceived/perceived and how it is possible to realize in principle a potentially infinite range of boundaried spaces and perspectives over an unlimited range of time.

4. I must emphasize that the N-N relations do not imply mere chance or random associations according to some empiricist "law." Nor are they, nor can they be, totally determinate and controlled. There is always, I maintain, a mixture of chance and control. The lower organism is relatively controlled, the human organism enjoys relative freedom of choice (see Merrell, 1980b, Chapter 3).

5. For further discussion see Merrell (1980c) where I use the term "metaparadigmatic framework," and Merrell (1981b) where I use "somewhere else," both terms being comparable to the "metaperspectival framework." Compare also the "metaperspectival framework" to what Lilly (1977) calls the "metabelief operator." Quite by chance I read Lilly after finishing the first draft of this inquiry and was surprised by the affinities between the results of his experiments and my theoretical framework.

4. When Are Boundaried Spaces Real?

1. Notice the similarity between Churchill-as-a-bulldog and the drawing of a unicorn in contrast to the face-as-Nixon. The face refers solely to one object in the physical world. The caricature, on the other hand, consists in bulldog-parts plus Churchill-parts, just as the unicorn is the combination of horse plus horn. However, there is also a crucial difference here. By establishing a continuity where a discontinuity would otherwise be perceived, the metaphor's mixture of parts constitutes it as a metaphor. In contrast, the unicorn, properly an imaginary beast, must be conceived as

the ordinarily contradictory and disjoint union of two existent physical world objects, for it does not satisfy the conditions for metaphoricity (cf. 2.25).

2. What I am speaking of here pertains to Peirce's idea concerning the formation of "habit," a generalizing tendency that ultimately terminates in a belief and a propensity toward action of a particular sort commensurate with that belief. Habit, according to Peirce, plays such an important role in all cognition and perception as to be "that specialization of the law of mind whereby a general idea gains the power of exciting reactions."

5. Toward a Model for the Generation of Time

1. In other words, Derrida's (1967) separation of the signifier from its signified to conceptualize an ethereal, autonomous, and referenceless domain of signifiers in incessant change is, I believe, a reality, though for "proper" communication signs must be used either directly or indirectly "as if" they had temporal footing in the domain of signifieds.

2. Of course, it has been demonstrated that the brain engaged in different activities puts out wave pulses of varying frequencies. The notion that the brain operates as a wave function parallels the discovery of modern physics that all natural phenomena, from galactic domains to subnuclear particles, are governed by periodic wave functions. It seems, therefore, reasonable to propose, and indeed there has recently been considerable speculation as well as empirical study along these lines by psychologists, philosophers, computer scientists, and physicists, that, at the lower levels, the cerebral cortex, and at the higher levels, the mind, can be described in terms of wave patterns (Bohm, 1971, 1979; de Valois, Albrecht and Thorell, 1978; Pribram, 1981). In a similar vein, concerning the relationship between states of consciousness and the "physical" world as it is known (hypothesized) by contemporary science and by Eastern and Western mystics, see, for example, Lilly (1967), Ornstein (1972), Ornstein, ed. (1973), LeShan (1974), Targ and Puthoff, eds. (1977), White, ed. (1974), and Young and Muses, eds. (1972). What I propose below, however, is purely formal and disengaged from the inconclusive empirical evidence we have at this time, although the future could certainly falsify or substantiate my conjectural hypothesis.

3. Concerning this "unit of time," Wiener (1948, 198) tells us that:

As is well known, when a visual signal arrives, the musuclar activity which it stimulates does not occur at once, but after a certain delay. . . . [T]his delay is not constant, but seems to consist of three parts. One of these parts is of constant length, whereas the other two appear to be uniformly distributed over about 1/10 second. It is as if the central nervous system could pick up incoming impulses only every 1/10 second, and as if the outgoing impulses to the muscles could arrive from the central nervous system only every 1/10 second. This is experimental evidence of a gating [i.e., like the logical circuits in computers]; and the association of this gating with 1/10 second, which is the approximate period of the central alpha rhythm of the brain, is very probably not fortuitous.

The phenomenon Wiener refers to is comparable to what James (1967, 292-301) calls the "pulses of experience" that become a continuity in consciousness.

4. Wiener's (1948, 199) comparison of brain activity to an oscillator must be mentioned at this point, and, I believe, it merits full citation:

> It is important to observe that if the frequency of an oscillator can be changed by impulses of a different frequency, the mechanism must be non-linear. A linear mechanism acting on an oscillation of a given frequency can produce only oscillation of the same frequency, generally with some change of phase and amplitude. This is not true for non-linear mechanisms, which may produce oscillations of frequencies which are the sum and differences of different orders, of the frequency of the oscillator and the frequency of the imposed disturbance. It is quite possible for such a mechanism to displace a frequency; and in the case which we have considered, this displacement will be of the nature of an attraction. It is not too improbable that this attraction will be along-time or secular phenomenon, and that for short times this system will remain approximately linear.
>
> Consider the possibility that the brain contains a number of oscillators of frequencies of nearly 10 per second, and that within limitations these frequencies can be attracted to one another. Under such circumstances, the frequencies are likely to be pulled together into one or more little clumps, at least in certain regions of the spectrum. The frequencies that are pulled into these clumps will have to be pulled away from somewhere, thus causing gaps in the spectrum, where the power is lower than that which we should otherwise expect. That such a phenomenon may actually take place in the generation of brain waves for the individual . . . is suggested by the sharp drop in the power for frequencies above 9.0 cycles per second.

5. See Cassirer (1953, 222). Also, compare this idea to Bohm (1951, 69), who speculates that there is an analogy between (1) "the instantaneous state of a thought with the position of a [an atomic] particle," and (2) "the general direction of change of that thought with the particle's momentum." Bohm's analogy embodies Heisenberg's indeterminacy principle as well as the wave function of matter. In addition, I believe that the hypothesis developed here is, in the final analysis, commensurate with Peirce's idea that there can be no intuition or cognition that is not determined by previous cognitions. In this sense the coming of awareness of a new item of experience "is never an instantaneous affair, but is an *event* occupying time, and coming to pass by a continuous process. Its prominence in consciousness, therefore must probably be the consummation of a growing process; and if so, there is no sufficient cause for the thought which had been the leading one just before, to cease abruptly and instantaneously" (Peirce, 1960, 5.284). In other words, consciousness (or mind processes) is in the Peircean sense defined as a continuum, while unrelated sensations (mind-states, and ultimately brain-states) can be defined either in terms of continuity or discontinuity, according to a given perspective.

6. Similarly, for Husserl (1964) there can be no isolated "instant" of time

in consciousness, for time is a "phasing in," an incessant movement of "protentional" and "retentional" traces. The present, then, necessarily includes phases of past as well as future.

6. Parts and Wholes

1. Note the similarity between Vygotsky's hypothesis here and the recent notion that the child's first speech is "telegraphic" (R. Brown, 1970, 1973; Piaget, 1952) or "holophrastic" (Bruner, 1967; Bloom, 1970, 1973; McNeill, 1966).

2. For further elaboration see Merrell (1980b).

3. For a summary of empirical studies along these lines see Neisser (1967).

4. Admittedly, the example of visual perception I have given has its counterpart in phonetics where "bits" of "noise" can be put in place of meaningful "bits" of information on a tape, then the hearer perceives the discourse on the tape with no awareness of the flaws (for example, Fodor and Bever, 1965; Warren, 1976). The distinction between auditory and visual perception will, however, become more evident below.

5. See Polanyi (1958) for further elaboration of "tacit knowing." It bears mentioning here that this chapter, and indeed much of this entire study, is influenced by Polanyi's notion of the "tacit dimension" as well as "focal" and "subsidiary" (which I usually call "peripheral") attention.

6. Along these lines, see, for example, such diverse thinkers as Bateson (1972), Neisser (1967), Peirce (1960), Polanyi (1958), and Schrödinger (1958).

7. Learning to Learn

1. There is a difference between *condensation* and *embedment*. *Embedment* of one space "into" another space generates a new meaning, but over time the organism tends to become less and less conscious of the original meaning. *Condensation* is the merging together of two or more interdependent and interrelated concatenated spaces into a larger space.

2. It now becomes evident how the theory of induction can arise by the assumption of repeated events, until finally the organism conceives of an event in the general, universal sense. However, the very important fact remains that initially something must be perceived as such-and-such before subsequent perception of similarity or identity is possible. Attempting to account for this origin with the theory of induction entails an infinite regress. Rather than perception and conception of universals being inductive, according to Popper's (1963) alternative, they represent the successive elaboration, hypothetico-deductively, of a limited set of inborn expectations (also called "hypotheses" by Popper).

3. It has undoubtedly been observed at this point that the combination of two similar, but not identical, signs to form a molecular sign entails embedment or nesting. Such nesting is necessary since the unrelated image of a "horse + horn," an icon in the Peircean sense, is, when given a name, incorporated into a larger image, that which is linked to "unicorn." The outer image, necessarily containing the inner one, is related to that inner image by similarity, and hence, without its name, it is a *hypoicon* (Peirce,

1960, 2.276). It is still a "First," for it does not yet entail the idea of what it is *not* (i.e., its *other,* or the "Second").

4. Peirce (1960, 2.277) tells us that *hypoicons* that represent their object by a parallelism to something else are *metaphors.* An "irregular pearl" is for obvious reasons a fitting image for what became known as the baroque. The additional characteristic of the nesting in operation (2) is the fading out of consciousness of the *hypoiconic* quality of the sign to become a "dead" metaphor ordinarily conceived like a Peircean symbol, or logosign.

5. Of course, this "machine model" entails, in the beginning, the proposition: "The universe is (like) a machine." Nevertheless, its image is appropriately an icon. Peirce (1960, 2.291) maintains that an icon "asserts nothing. If an icon could be interpreted by a sentence, that sentence must be in a 'potential mood,' that is, it would merely say, 'Suppose a figure has three sides,' etc." From an icon, or *hypoicon* in this case, a primitive proposition, "The universe is (like) a machine" can be generated. This proposition contains, as a potential to be actualized, all the successive propositions from within the Cartesian-Newtonian framework (see Merrell, 1980b, for discussion of such a potential). Furthermore, it can be observed, with respect to these successive propositions implied by the operation in (3), that the *hypoiconic* metaphorical parallelism has become embedded in consciousness such that, unlike operation (2), the image is retained while the parallelism, rather than resting in something else, is incorporated into the referred object itself.

6. The illustrations that follow are not meant to be "proofs." They are the basic form of a "logic" of boundaried space embedment and de-embedment in human consciousness. Compare, however, these illustrations with Laing's (1969) use of set theory in psychoanalysis, with the notion of "logical nets" developed as a model of the brain (summarized in George, 1962), and with Peirce's rules of iteration and deiteration in his "existential graphs" (see Roberts, 1973).

Moreover, the process of embedment and de-embedment outlined here, although much simpler than the "existential graphs" since it deals exclusively with automatization in consciousness, is nonetheless compatible with Peirce's thought. In fact, my formulation contains, I believe, the seeds of his notion concerning what logic should be. This becomes evident in one of Peirce's letters to Lady Welby wherein he states that the "most generally useful rules [of 'existential graphs'] are those of Iteration (in evenly enclosed areas) and Deiteration (from oddly enclosed areas), and the Rule of the Double Cut" (Hardwick, ed., 1977, 96). Notice the similarity between Peirce's terms and the above axioms as well as the notion of boundaried spaces.

7. This does not indicate that I am endorsing the "logical justification" theory of knowledge propounded by the logical positivists (see 0.12). Progressive embedment (*condensation*) of spaces implies expanded tacit awareness of conceptual frameworks. For this reason it appears that these (*condensed*) spaces are reducible to an axiomatic set of atomic propositions from which all knowledge in that conceptual framework is derived. Nevertheless, these atomic propositions do not stand alone, but they are necessarily related to other propositions, statements, and spaces in ever-larger systems. This notion is compatible with Peirce's "indefinite semiosis," which allows for no ultimate starting point (see Eco, 1976, 1979).

8. Aspects of a Viable Theory of Texts

1. "Trial-and-error elimination" is not to be related to an oversimplified form of behaviorism. We must keep in mind that the organism begins with a set of inborn expectations and, by a hypothetico-deductive process, constantly develops new expectations when old expectations remain unsatisfied. "Trial-and-error elimination," then, entails the organism's rejection of one expectation in favor of another, and the "testing" of it in the organism's environment until it, also, remains unsatisfied. The chief difference between the human and the animal organism is, it must be emphasized, that the former learns consciously and actively to seek out new expectations and to discover error in old expectations (in general, see Popper, 1963, 1972, 1974).

2. See also Piaget's (1972) studies that demonstrate how children, as their mental structures develop, are able to recognize "laws" upon which they later act, even in the face of counterfactual evidence.

3. Of course these "marks-on-paper" cannot be considered completely static. Loss of portions of a manuscript, spelling errors and typos, errata during printing, reprinting and re-editing, etc., as well as problems of translation, introduce an inevitable degree of variation.

4. I must reemphasize that I by no means propose that oral cultures are to be discounted. The thrust of this inquiry resting on the nature of written texts, however, demands focus on the difference, though most apparently of degree rather than kind, between written and oral texts.

Actually, as Schwegler (1980) points out after a study of Renaissance England, when oral and literate cultures coexisted, there was mutually influential interaction between them such that the first brought about frequent stylistic and structural changes in the second. The two traditions, to repeat, are complementary, yet dynamically so.

9. The Semiotic Web

1. I am not necessarily propounding the speculatory notion that there may be parallels between the binary ("digital") nature of the genetic code and human speech (Beadle and Beadle, 1966; Gerard, Kluckhohn and Rapoport, 1956; Masters, 1970; Sebeok, 1963), that Western world phonetic-based writing, as opposed to other forms of writing in other cultures, is founded on the same pattern and that, therefore, the genetic code may be the "primary manifestation of both life and language" (Jakobson, 1973). I am simply stating what appears to be the case according to the hierarchical system I am constructing.

2. *Words, statements* and *texts* can be compared to Peirce's (1960, 1.559) triadic division of symbols:

(a) "Symbols which directly determine only their *grounds* or imputed qualities, and are thus but sums of marks or *terms*" (the counterpart to *words*).

(b) "Symbols which also independently determine their *objects* by means of other term or terms, and thus, expressing their own objective validity, become capable of truth or falsehood, that is, are *propositions*" (the counterpart to *statements*).

(c) "Symbols which also independently determine their *interpretants,* and thus the minds to which they appeal, by premissing a proposition or propositions which such a mind is to admit. These are *arguments*" (the counterpart to *texts*—except that the text's premise can, and usually does, remain implicit, due to inevitable *embedment*).

3. The use of boundaried spaces as counterparts to Peirce's icons is significant here. Peirce (1960, 2.278) tells us that: "The only way of directly communicating an idea is by means of an icon; and every indirect method of communicating an idea must depend for its establishment upon the use of an icon. Hence every assertion must contain an icon or set of icons, or else must contain signs whose meanings are only explicable by icons." And the combining of these boundaried spaces-as-icons within syntactically structured strings of symbols follows Peircean logic, for he maintains that icons "of the algebraic kind, though usually very simple ones, exist in all ordinary grammatical propositions. . . . In all primitive writing, such as the Egyptian hieroglyphics, there are icons of a non-logical kind, the ideographs. In the earliest form of speech, there probably was a large element of mimicry. But in all languages known, such representations have been replaced by conventional auditory signs. These, however, are such that they can only be explained by icons" (Peirce, 1960, 2.280).

4. I have fused two boundaried spaces to form a larger, more complex boundaried space in such a manner that the spaces, possessing iconic properties, conjoin to produce a larger and continuous (or "analog") image (icon) the explicit articulation of which entails a proposition. Signs, according to Peirce, come in varying degrees of complexity. For example: "A sign may have more than one Object. Thus, the sentence 'Cain killed Abel,' which is a Sign, refers at least as much to Abel as to Cain, even if it be not regarded as it should, as having 'a *killing*' as a third Object. But the set of objects may be regarded as making up one complex Object." And further: "If a sign is other than its Object, there must exist, either in thought or in expression, some explanation or argument or other context, showing how— upon what system or for what reason the Sign represents the Object or set of Objects that it does. Now the Sign and the Explanation together make up another Sign, and since the explanation will be a Sign, it will probably require an additional explanation, which taken together with the already enlarged Sign will make up a still larger Sign; and proceeding in the same way, we shall, or should, ultimately reach a Sign of itself, containing its own explanation and those of all significant parts; and according to this explanation each such part has some other part as its Object" (Peirce, 1960, 2.230). The icon, then, holistic and continuous in form, can, according to its complexity, contain the potential for an indefinitely long string of articulated or written symbols. This notion will have a bearing on later stages of this inquiry.

5. That linear, syntactic arrangements of symbols can become, in consciousness, transformed into iconic clusters and vice versa is commensurate, once again, with Peircean thought. Symbols are never static, they grow. "They come into being by development out of other signs, particularly from icons, or from mixed signs partaking of the nature of icons and symbols" (Peirce, 1960, 2.302).

In addition, and with respect to the formulations in 9.23, elsewhere (Merrell, 1981b, 1981d) I have expounded on what I believe to be, at an exceedingly deep level, the most basic operation by means of which something is distinguished (i.e., *differentiated*) from something else. This operation is derived from Peirce's "logic of relatives" and his "existential graphs" (see Roberts, 1973), from Sheffer's "stroke function" (see Whitehead and Russell, 1927), and from Spencer-Brown's (1969) "mark of distinction."

6. It bears stating that I do not propose the prelogic/logic dichotomy between "primitive" and "modern" cultures (as do Lévy-Bruhl and others). The thinking of "primitives" may well be as sophisticated as that of the "moderns." The latters' apparent advantage is that their media differs and therefore their opportunities for diversity. Witness the "knowledge explosion" in this age of computers that makes available to us a tremendous range of possibilities unavailable to all previous generations. Moreover, future possibilities as a result of computer technology and interaction between the human mind and computers are at this time unpredictable. Such possibility for diversity, for change, is completely unknown in the so-called "primitive" cultures.

7. Significantly, Wilden (1972, 407) points out that with respect to an oral culture:

> without writing as such, the past of the society—its memory, its set of instructions, its sacred text—is literally embodied in every domicile, in every person or group who exemplifies a ritual or who recalls a myth. Except insofar as the ground plan of the village and/or various cultural objects and implements provide a minimal objective memory for the survival of the organization of the society from generation to generation, the significant distinctions in such a society have to be maintained, reconstructed, represented, and, in essence, RE-INVENTED in the very flesh of each generation.

In contrast, as we shall observe, the existence of writing and texts in literate cultures dramatically accelerates the possibilities of analysis, of recognizing error, and of changing human thought. Literate societies, in other words, enjoy vastly greater semiotic freedom.

8. See, in this respect, the "paradigm" view of scientific theories as discussed above. For the notion of language, philosophic, religious, etc. "paradigms" or "forms of life" in a more general sense, see Laszlo (1972), MacCormac (1976), Phillips (1973, 1975), Trigg (1973), Whorf (1956), Wittgenstein (1953, 1966, 1969). For a synthesis of these views into a "metaframework," see Merrell (1978a).

10. Text and Countertext

1. See Merrell (1981b) for further discussion of *difference* in light of Derrida's notion of *Difference*.

2. This *bricoleur*/engineer dichotomy from Lévi-Strauss is admittedly an oversimplification. Elsewhere (Merrell, 1981b) I elaborate on the *bricoleur* in the modern scientist as well as the engineer in the "primitive" mind. Yet, as will become evident in Chapter 11, there is a degree of truth to the notion that in traditional cultures man lives *within* his world, while Westerners set themselves *apart from* their world.

3. It is important to note also that in the Peircean sense thoughts (or sign

systems) are not truly meaningful without counterthoughts (and counter-sign systems). Moreover, all knowledge presupposes prior knowledge; otherwise it could not be said that there is any "accumulation of knowledge."

11. Concerning the Real Nature of Texts

1. This assertion stems from the well-known theorem of Gödel (see Nagel and Newman, 1964; also Merrell, 1978a).

2. This de-embedment of texts goes by the name of "deconstruction" in Derridean circles. While "deconstruction" is obviously one method of de-embedment, albeit a rather unidirectional one, it is not necessarily the method advocated here (for a critique of "deconstruction" see Merrell, 1981b). In fact, no method is proposed here; I am solely attempting to get at the underlying reality of texts.

REFERENCES

Abbott, Edwin A.
    1952. *Flatland*. New York: Dover Publications.
Altmann, Stuart
    1962. "Social Behavior of Anthropoid Primates: Analysis of Recent Con-
    cepts." In *Roots of Behavior: Genetics, Instinct, and Socialization in Animal
    Behavior*, ed. E. L. Bliss, pp. 277–85. New York: Harper & Row.
Ardrey, Robert
    1967. *The Territorial Imperative*. London: Collins.
Arnheim, Rudolf
    1969. *Visual Thinking*. Berkeley: University of California Press.
Bartlett, F. C.
    1958. *Thinking*. New York: Basic Books.
Bateson, Gregory
    1972. *Steps to an Ecology of Mind*. New York: Chandler Publishing Co.
    1977. "Afterword." In *About Bateson*, ed. J. Brockman, pp. 235–47. New
    York: E. P. Dutton.
Beadle, George, and Beadle, Muriel
    1966. *The Language of Life*. Garden City, New York: Doubleday & Co.
Bentov, Itzhak
    1977. *Stalking the Wild Pendulum: On the Mechanics of Consciousness*. New
    York: E. P. Dutton.
Berger, Peter L., and Luckmann, Thomas
    1967. *The Social Construction of Reality*. Garden City, New York: Double-
    day & Co.
Berggren, D.
    1962/63. "The Use and Abuse of Metaphor I," and "The Use and Abuse
    of Metaphor II." *Review of Metaphysics* 16: 236–58, 450–72.
Bernstein, Basil
    1975. *Class, Codes and Control: Theoretical Studies Towards a Sociology of
    Language*. New York: Schocken Books, Inc.
Bertalanffy, Ludwig von
    1967. *Robots, Men and Minds*. New York: George Braziller.
Black, Max
    1962. *Models and Metaphors*. Ithaca: Cornell University Press.
Bloom, Lois M.
    1970. *Language Development: Form and Function in Emerging Grammars*.
    Cambridge: The M. I. T. Press.
    1973. *One Word at a Time: The Use of Single Word Utterances before Syntax*.
    The Hague: Mouton.
Bloor, David
    1976. *Knowledge and Social Imagery*. London: Routledge & Kegan Paul.
Bogen, J. E.
    1969. "The Other Side of the Brain, II: An Appositional Mind." *Bulletin
    of the Los Angeles Neurological Society* 34: 135–62.

Bogen, J. E., and Bogen, G. M.

1969. "The Other Side of the Brain, III: The Corpus Callosum and Creativity." *Bulletin of the Los Angeles Neurological Society* 34: 191–220.

Bohm, David

1951. *Quantum Theory.* New York: Prentice-Hall.

1957. *Causality and Chance in Modern Physics.* Philadelphia: University of Pennsylvania Press.

1971. "Quantum Theory as an Indication of a New Order in Physics. Part A: The Derivation of New Orders as Shown through the History of Physics." *Foundations of Physics* 1: 359–81.

1979. *A Question of Physics: Conversations in Physics and Biology.* Conducted by P. Buckley and F. D. Peat, pp. 124–50. Toronto: University of Toronto Press.

Bohr, Neils

1958. *Atomic Physics and Human Knowledge.* New York: John Wiley & Sons.

Boler, John P.

1964. "Habits of Thought." In *Studies in the Philosophy of Charles Sanders Peirce,* ed. E. C. Moore and R. S. Robin, pp. 382–400. Amherst: The University of Massachusetts Press.

Borges, Jorge Luis

1964. *Labyrinths, Selected Stories and Other Writings.* Edited by D. A. Yates and J. E. Irby. New York: New Directions.

Brentano, Franz Clemens

1973. *Psychology from an Empirical Standpoint.* Translated by A. C. Rencorello, D. B. Terrell, and L. L. McAlister. London: Routledge & Kegan Paul.

Bridgman, Percy W.

1959. *The Way Things Are.* Cambridge: Harvard University Press.

Bronowski, Jacob

1967. "Human and Animal Language." In *To Honor Roman Jakobson,* ed. T. Sebeok, vol. 1, pp. 427–46. 3 vols. The Hague: Mouton.

1978. *The Origins of Knowledge and Imagination.* New Haven: Yale University Press.

Bronowski, J. and Bellugi, Ursula

1970. "Language, Name, and Concept." *Science* 168, 669–73.

Brown, Harold I.

1977. *Perception, Theory and Commitment: The New Philosophy of Science.* Chicago: The University of Chicago Press.

Brown, Roger

1970. "The First Sentences of Child and Chimpanzee." In *Psycholinguistics: Selected Papers,* pp. 208–31. New York: Free Press.

1973. *A First Language: The Early Stages.* Cambridge: Harvard University Press.

Bruner, Jerome S.

1957. "Going Beyond the Information Given." In *Contemporary Approaches to Cognition: A Symposium Held at the University of Colorado,* pp. 41–69. Cambridge: Harvard University Press.

1962. *On Knowing: Essays for the Left Hand.* Cambridge: The Belknap Press of Harvard University Press.

1967. "The Ontogenesis of Symbols." In *To Honor Roman Jakobson,* ed. T. Sebeok, vol. 1, pp. 447–67. 3 vols. The Hague: Mouton.

Bruner, J. S., and Postman, Leo
1949. "On the Perception of Incongruity: A Paradigm." *Journal of Personality* 18, 206–23.

Bühler, Karl
1934. *Sprachtheorie.* Jena: Fischer.

Butler, Samuel
1913. *Life and Habit.* London: Jonathan Cape.

Caillois, Roger
1969. *Man and the Sacred.* Translated by M. Barash. Glencoe, Illinois: The Free Press.

Callan, Hilary
1970. *Ethology and Society.* London: The Clarendon Press.

Capek, Milic
1961. *The Philosophical Impact of Contemporary Physics.* New York: American Book Co.

Capra, Fritjof
1975. *The Tao of Physics.* Berkeley: Shambhala Publishers.

Carnap, Rudolf
1966. *An Introduction to the Philosophy of Science.* Edited by M. Gardner. New York: Basic Books.

Cassirer, Ernst
1946. *Language and Myth.* Translated by S. K. Langer. New York: Dover Publications.
1953. *The Philosophy of Symbolic Forms,* vol. I. Translated by R. Manheim. New Haven: Yale University Press.

Chomsky, Noam
1965. *Aspects of the Theory of Syntax.* Cambridge: The M. I. T. Press.
1968. *Language and Mind.* New York: Harcourt, Brace & World.
1972. *Reflections on Language.* New York: Pantheon Books.

Count, Earl W.
1969. "Animal Communication in Man-Science: An Essay in Perspective." In *Approaches to Animal Communication,* ed. T. Sebeok, pp. 77–130. The Hague: Mouton.

Crick, Malcolm
1976. *Explorations in Language and Meaning: Towards a Semantic Anthropology.* London: Malaby Press.

Culler, Jonathan
1975. *Structuralist Poetics.* Ithaca; Cornell University Press.

Derrida, Jacques
1967. *De la Grammatologie.* Paris: Minuit.

DeValois, Russell L.; Albrecht, Duane G.; and Thorell, Lisa G.
1978. "Cortical Cells: Bar and Edge Detectors, or Spatial Frequency Filters?" In *Frontiers in Visual Science,* ed. S. Cool and E. L. Smith, pp. 544–56. New York: Springer-Verlag.

Dijk, Teun van
1972. *Some Aspects of Text-Grammars: A Study in the Foundations of Theoretical Poetics.* The Hague: Mouton.

Dobzhansky, Theodosius
1967. *The Biology of Ultimate Concern.* New York: The New American Library.

Douglas, Mary
1966. *Purity and Danger: An Analysis of Concepts of Pollution and Taboo.* New York: Praeger.
1973. *Natural Symbols.* New York: Random House.
Duhem, Pierre
1962. *The Aim and Structure of Physical Theory.* Translated by P. P. Wiener. New York: Atheneum.
Eco, Umberto
1976. *A Theory of Semiotics.* Bloomington: Indiana University Press.
1979. *The Role of the Reader: Explorations in the Semiotics of Texts.* Bloomington: Indiana University Press.
Ehrmann, Jacques
1971. "*Homo Ludens* Revisited." In *Game, Play, Literature,* ed. J. Ehrmann pp. 31–57. Boston: Beacon Press.
Fernandez, James
1974. "The Mission of Metaphor in Expressive Culture." *Cultural Anthropology* 15, No. 2, 119–45.
1980. "Edification by Puzzlement." In *Explorations in African Systems of Thought,* ed. I. Karp and C. S. Bird, pp. 44–59. Bloomington: Indiana University Press.
Feyerabend, Paul
1975. *Against Method.* London: NLB.
Findlay, J. N.
1963. *Meinong's Theory of Objects and Values.* Oxford: The Clarendon Press.
Floyd, Keith
1974. "Of Time and Mind: From Paradox to Paradigm." In *Frontiers of Consciousness,* ed. J. White, pp. 296–320. New York: Avon Books.
Fodor, J. A., and Bever, T. G.
1965. "The Psychological Reality of Linguistic Segments." *Journal of Verbal Learning and Verbal Behavior* 4: 414–20.
Fouts, Roger S., and Rigby, Randall L.
1977. "Man-Chimpanzee Communication." In *How Animals Communicate,* ed. T. Sebeok, pp. 1034–54. Bloomington: Indiana University Press.
Fry, William F.
1963. *Sweet Madness: A Study of Humor.* Palo Alto, California: Pacific Books.
Gardner, R. Allen, and Gardner, Beatrice
1969. "Teaching Sign-Language to a Chimpanzee." *Science* 165: 664–72.
Gazzinaga, M.
1970. *The Bisected Brain.* New York: Appleton-Century-Crofts.
George, Frank Honywill
1962. *The Brain as a Computer.* Oxford: Pergamon Press.
Gerard, R.; Kluckhohn, C.; and Rapoport, A.
1956. "Biological and Cultural Evolution: Some Analogies and Explorations." *Behavioral Sciences* 1: 234–51.
Gombrich, E. G.
1960. *Art and Illusion.* Princeton: Princeton University Press.
Goodman, Nelson
1972. *Problems and Projects.* Indianapolis: The Bobbs-Merrill Company.
1976. *Languages of Art: An Approach to a Theory of Symbols.* Indianapolis: Hackett Publishing Co.
1978. *Ways of Worldmaking.* Indianapolis: Hackett Publishing Co.

Goody, Jack
1977. *The Domestication of the Savage Mind*. Cambridge: Cambridge University Press.
Gregory, R. L.
1966. *Eye and Brain: The Psychology of Seeing*. New York: McGraw-Hill.
1970. *The Intelligent Eye*. New York: McGraw-Hill.
Grene, Marjorie
1974. *The Understanding of Nature: Essays in the Philosophy of Biology*. Dordrecht-Holland: D. Reidel.
Groot, Adriaan D.
1966. "Perception and Memory versus Thought: Some Old Ideas and Recent Findings." In *Problem Solving*, ed. B. Klienmuntz, pp. 19–50. New York: John Wiley.
Hadamard, Jacques
1945. *The Psychology of Invention in the Mathematical Field*. New York: Dover Publications.
Hall, Edward T.
1976. *Beyond Culture*. New York: Doubleday & Co.
Hanson, F. Allen
1979. "Does God Have a Body? Truth, Reality and Cultural Relativism." *Man* 14, No. 3, 515–29.
Hanson, Norwood R.
1958. *Patterns of Discovery*. Cambridge: Cambridge University Press.
1965. "Notes Toward a Logic of Discovery." In *Perspectives on Peirce*, ed. R. J. Bernstein, pp. 42–65. New Haven: Yale University Press.
Hardwick, Charles S., ed.
1977. *Semiotic and Significs: The Correspondence between Charles S. Peirce and Victoria Lady Welby*. Bloomington: Indiana University Press.
Hausman, Carl R.
1975. *A Discourse on Novelty and Creation*. The Hague: Martinus Nijhoff.
Hayek, F. A.
1969. "The Primacy of the Abstract." In *Beyond Reductionism: Perspectives in the Life Sciences*, ed. A. Koestler and J. R. Smithies, pp. 309–33. New York: MacMillan.
Heisenberg, Werner.
1958. *Physics and Philosophy*. New York: Harper & Row.
Helmholtz, Hermann Ludwig von
1971. *Selected Writings*. Middletown, Conn.: Wesleyan University Press.
Hempel, Carl G.
1965. *Aspects of Scientific Explanation*. New York: The Free Press.
Hesse, Mary
1966. *Models and Analogies in Science*. Notre Dame: University of Notre Dame Press.
Hewes, Gordon W.
1971. "An Explicit Formulation of the Relationships between Tool-Using, Tool-Making, and Emergence of Language." In *Abstracts, American Anthropological Association*, Annual Meeting: New York, American Anthropological Association.
1973. "Primate Communication, and the Gestural Origin of Language." *Current Anthropology* 14, No. 1/2, 5-24.

Hockett, Charles F.
1959. "Animal 'Languages' and Human Language." In *The Evolution of Man's Capacity for Culture,* ed. J. N. Spuhler, pp. 32–39. Detroit: Wayne State University Press.

Hockett, C. F., and Ascher, R.
1964. "The Human Revolution." *Current Anthropology* 5, No. 3, 135–47.

Hofstadter, Douglas R.
1979. *Gödel, Escher, Bach: An Eternal Golden Braid.* New York: Basic Books.

Horton, Robin
1967. "African Traditional Thought and Western Science." *Africa* 37: 50–71, 155–87.

Howell, Robert
1979. "Fictional Objects: How They Are and How They Aren't." *Poetics* 8, No. 1/2, 129–77.

Huizinga, Johan
1955. *Homo Ludens.* Boston: Beacon Press.

Husserl, Edmund
1964. *The Phenomenology of Internal Time-Consciousness.* Translated by J. S. Churchill. Bloomington: Indiana University Press.

Jakobson, Roman
1960. "Linguistics and Poetics." In *Style in Language,* ed. T. Sebeok, pp. 350–77. Cambridge: The M. I. T. Press.
1973. *Main Trends in the Science of Language.* London: George Allen & Unwin.

Jakobson, R.; Fant, G. G. M.; and Halle, M.
1964. *Preliminaries to Speech Analysis.* Cambridge: The M. I. T. Press.

Jakobson, Roman, and Halle, Morris
1956. *Fundamentals of Language.* The Hague: Mouton.

James, William
1967. *The Writings of William James.* New York: Random House.

Jarvie, I. C., and Agassi, J.
1967. "The Rationality of Magic." *British Journal of Sociology* 18: 55–74.
1973. "Magic and Rationality Again." *British Journal of Sociology* 24: 236–45.

Klir, Jiri, and Valach, Miroslav
1967. *Cybernetic Modelling.* Translated by W. A. Ainsworth. London: D. Van Nostrand.

Koestler, Arthur
1964. *The Act of Creation.* New York: Dell Publishing Co.
1971. *The Ghost in the Machine.* Chicago: Henry Regnery.

Kuhn, Thomas S.
1970. *The Structure of Scientific Revolutions.* Chicago: The University of Chicago Press.

Kuhns, Richard
1970. *Structures of Experience.* New York: Harper & Row.

Labov, William
1972. *Language in the Inner City: Studies in the Black English Vernacular.* Philadelphia: University of Pennsylvania Press.

Laing, R. D.
1967. *The Politics of Experience.* New York: Ballantine Books.
1969. *The Politics of the Family.* New York: Random House.

Lashley, K. S.

1951. "The Problem of Serial Order in Behavior." In *Cerebral Mechanisms in Behavior: The Hixon Symposium*, ed. L. A. Jeffreys, pp. 112–36. New York: John Wiley.

Laszlo, Ervin

1972. *Introduction to Systems Philosophy*. New York: Harper & Row.

Leach, Edmund

1964. "Anthropological Aspects of Language: Animal Categories and Verbal Abuse." In *New Directions in the Study of Language*, ed. E. H. Lenneberg, pp. 23–63. Cambridge: The M. I. T. Press.

1976. *Culture and Communication*. Cambridge: Cambridge University Press.

Leatherdale, W. H.

1974. *The Role of Analogy: Model and Metaphor in Science*. Amsterdam: North-Holland Publishing Co.

Lee, Dorothy

1959. *Freedom and Culture*. New York: Prentice-Hall.

Lenneberg, Eric H.

1967. *Biological Foundations of Language*. New York: John Wiley.

LeShan, Lawrence

1974. *The Medium, the Mystic, and the Physicist: Toward a General Theory of the Paranormal*. New York: The Viking Press.

Lévi-Strauss, Claude

1963. *Structural Anthropology*. Translated by C. Jacobson and B. G. Schoepf. New York: Doubleday & Co.

1966. *The Savage Mind*. Chicago: The University of Chicago Press.

1969. *The Raw and the Cooked*. Translated by J. and D. Weightman. New York: Harper & Row.

Lilly, John C.

1967. *Programming and Metaprogramming in the Human Biocomputer*. New York: Julian Press.

1977. *The Deep Self*. New York: Warner Books.

Linden, Eugene

1976. *Apes, Men, and Language*. London: Penguin Books.

Loizos, C.

1967. "Play Behaviour in Higher Primates: A Review." In *Primate Ethology*, ed. D. Morris, pp. 176–218. London: Weidenfeld & Nicolson.

Lorenz, K. Z.

1966. *On Aggression*. London: Methuen.

Luria, Aleksandr Romanovich

1968. *The Mind of the Mnemonist*. Translated by L. Solotaroff. New York: Basic Books.

McClosky, M.

1964. "Metaphors." *Mind* 73: 215–33.

MacCormac, Earl R.

1976. *Metaphor and Myth in Science and Religion*. Durham: Duke University Press.

McCulloch, Warren Sturgis

1965. "What the Frog's Eye Tells the Frog's Brain." In *Embodiments of Mind*, by W. S. McCulloch, pp. 230–50. Cambridge: The M. I. T. Press.

McKenna, Terence, and McKenna, Dennis

1975. *The Invisible Landscape: Mind, Hallucinogens and the I Ching*. New York: Seabury Press.

McNeill, D.
  1966. "Developmental Psycholinguistics." In *The Genesis of Language,* ed.
  R. Smith and G. A. Miller, pp. 15–84. Cambridge: The M. I. T. Press.
Malcolm, Norman
  1971. *Problems of Mind: Descartes to Wittgenstein.* New York: Harper &
  Row.
Marler, Peter
  1977. "The Evolution of Communication." In *How Animals Communicate,*
  ed. T. Sebeok, pp. 45–70. Bloomington: Indiana University Press.
Masters, Roger D.
  1970. "Genes, Language, and Evolution." *Semiotica* 2, No. 4, 295–320.
Melhuish, George
  1973. *The Paradoxical Nature of Reality.* Bristol: St. Vincent's Press.
Merrell, Floyd
  1976a. "Communication and Paradox in Carlos Fuentes' *The Death of
  Artemio Cruz." Semiotica* 18, No. 4, 339–60.
  1976b. "Fearful Paradoxes (Dissymmetries)." In *Film Studies Annual,* ed.
  B. Lawton, et. al., pp. 52–73. West Lafayette, Indiana: Purdue Research
  Foundation.
  1978a. "Metaphor and Metonymy: A Key to Narrative Analysis." *Language and Style* 11, No. 3, 146–63.
  1978b. "How We Perceive Texts." *Dispositio* 3, No. 7–8, 167–73.
  1979. "Some Signs that Preceded their Times: Or, Are We Really Ready
  For Peirce?" *Ars Semeiotica* 2, No. 2, 149–72.
  1980a. "Of Metaphor and Metonymy." *Semiotica* 31, No. 3/4, 289–307.
  1980b. *Para-Realities: The Nature of Our Fictions and How We Know Them.*
  Amsterdam: John Benjamins, forthcoming.
  1980c. "A Semiotic Theory of Texts." Unpublished manuscript.
  1980d. "Understanding Fictions." *Kodikas/Code* 2, No. 3, 233–50.
  1981a. " On Understanding the Logic of Understanding." *Ars Semeiotica,*
  14, No. 2, 161–86.
  1981b. "Deconstruction in Perspective." Unpublished manuscript.
Morris, Desmond
  1967. *The Naked Ape.* London: Jonathan Cape.
Nagel, Ernest, and Newman, James R.
  1964. *Gödel's Proof.* New York: New York University Press.
Needham, Rodney
  1973. *Right and Left: Essays on Dual Symbolic Classification.* Chicago: The
  University of Chicago Press.
Neisser, Ulric
  1967. *Cognitive Psychology.* Englewood Cliffs: Prentice-Hall.
Neumann, J. von
  1958. *The Computer and the Brain.* New Haven: Yale University Press.
Ogden, C. K., and Richards, I. A.
  1923. *The Meaning of Meaning.* New York: Harcourt, Brace & World.
Ornstein, Robert
  1972. *The Psychology of Consciousness.* San Francisco: W. H. Freeman.
Ornstein, Robert, ed.
  1973. *The Nature of Human Consciousness.* San Francisco: W. H. Freeman.
Paivio, A.
  1971. *Imagery and Verbal Processes.* New York: Holt, Rinehart & Winston.

Paredes, J. A., and Hepburn, M. J.
1976. "The Split Brain and the Culture and Cognition Paradox." *Current Anthropology* 17: 121–27.

Parsons, Terence
1975. "A Meinongian Analysis of Fictional Objects." *Grazer Philosophische Studen* 1: 73–86.

Peirce, Charles Sanders
1958. *Collected Papers of Charles Sanders Peirce*. Vols. VII and VIII, ed. A. W. Burks. Cambridge: Harvard University Press.
1960. *Collected Papers of Charles Sanders Peirce*. Vols. I-VI, ed. C. Hartshorne and P. Weiss. Cambridge: The Belknap Press of Harvard University Press.

Pepper, Stephen C.
1942. *World Hypotheses*. Berkeley: University of California Press.

Phillips, Derek L.
1973. *Abandoning Method*. San Francisco: Jossey-Bass Publishers.
1975. "Paradigms and Incommensurability." *Theory and Society* 2, No. 1, 37–62.

Piaget, Jean
1926. *The Language and Thought of the Child*. London: K. Paul, Trench, Trubner & Co.
1952. *The Origins of Intelligence in Children*. New York: International Universities Press.
1969. *The Child's Conception of the World*. Translated by J. and A. Tomlinson. Totowa, New Jersey: Littlefield, Adams, & Co.
1972. *Psychology and Epistemology*. Translated by A. Rosin. New York: The Viking Press.
1973. *The Child and Reality*. Translated by A. Rosin. New York: The Viking Press.
1978. *Behavior and Evolution*. Translated by D. Nicholson-Smith. New York: Pantheon Books.

Polanyi, Michael
1958. *Personal Knowledge*. Chicago: The University of Chicago Press.
1964. *Science, Faith and Society*. Chicago: The University of Chicago Press.

Popper, Karl R.
1959. *The Logic of Scientific Discovery*. New York: Harper & Row.
1963. *Conjectures and Refutations*. New York: Harper & Row.
1972. *Objective Knowledge*. London: Oxford University Press.
1974. *Unended Quest: An Intellectual Autobiography*. La Salle, Illinois: Open Court.

Premack, David
1970. "The Education of Sarah: A Chimp Learns Language." *Psychology Today* 4, No. 4, 55–58.
1971. "Language in the Chimpanzee?" *Science* 172: 808–22.

Pribram, Karl H.
1971. *Languages of the Brain*. Englewood Cliffs: Prentice-Hall.
1981. "The Distributed Nature of the Memory Store and the Localization of Linguistic Competencies." In *Proceedings of a Symposium on: The Neurological Basis of Signs in Communication Processes*, ed. P. Perron, pp. 127–47. Toronto: Toronto Semiotic Circle Monographs, Working Papers and Prepublications.

Rescher, Nicholas
1973. *Conceptual Idealism.* Oxford: Basil Blackwell.
Roberts, Don D.
1973. *The Existential Graphs of Charles S. Peirce.* The Hague: Mouton.
Rosch, Eleanor
1974. "Linguistic Relativity." In *Human Communication: Perspectives,* ed.
A. Silverstein, pp. 95–121. New York: Halsted Press.
1978. "Principles of Categorization." In *Cognition and Categorization,* ed.
E. Rosch and B. B. Lloyd, pp. 28–48. Hillsdale: Lawrence Erlbaum.
Routley, Richard
1979. "The Semantical Structure of Fictional Discourse." *Poetics,* 8, No.
1/2, 3–30.
Ruesch, Jurgen, and Bateson, Gregory
1951. *Communication: The Social Matrix of Psychiatry.* New York: W. W.
Norton.
Rumbaugh, Duane M.
1977. *Language Learning by a Chimpanzee: The Lana Experiment.* New York:
Academic Press.
Russell, Bertrand
1956. *Logic and Knowledge: Essays, 1901–50.* Edited by R. C. Marsh. New
York: G. P. Putnam's Sons.
Ryle, Gilbert
1949. *The Concept of Mind.* New York: Harper & Row.
Saussure, Ferdinand de
1966. *Course in General Linguistics.* Translated by W. Baskin. New York:
McGraw-Hill.
Schlesinger, I. M.
1971. "Production of Utterances and Language Acquisition." In *The On-
togenesis of Grammar,* ed. D. I. Slobin, pp. 63–101. New York: Academic
Press.
Schrödinger, Erwin
1945. *What Is Life?* London: Cambridge Univeristy Press.
1958. *Mind And Matter.* London: Cambridge University Press.
Schwengler, Robert A.
1980. "Oral Tradition and Print: Domestic Performance in Renaissance
England." *Journal of American Folklore* 93, No. 370, 435–41.
Sebeok, Thomas A.
1963. "Communication among Social Bees; Porpoises and Sonar; Man
and Dolphin." *Language* 39: 448–66.
1972. *Perspectives in Zoosemiotics.* The Hague: Mouton.
1976a. "Iconicity." *Modern Language Notes* 91, No. 6, 1427–56.
1976b. *Contributions to the Doctrine of Signs.* Bloomington: Indiana University Press.
1979. *The Sign and Its Masters.* Austin: The University of Texas Press.
Sebeok, Thomas, A., ed.
1977. *A Perfusion of Signs.* Bloomington: Indiana University Press.
1978. *Sight, Sound, and Sense.* Bloomington: Indiana University Press.
1981. *The Clever Hans Phenomena: Communication with Horses, Whales, Apes,
and People.* New York: New York Academy of Sciences.
Simonds, Paul E.
1974. *The Social Primates.* New York: Harper & Row.

Singh, Jagjit
1966. *Great Ideas in Information Theory, Language and Cybernetics.* New York: Dover Publications.
Smith, David W.
1975. "Meinongian Objects." *Grazer Philosophische Studen* 1: 43–72.
Spencer-Brown, G.
1969. *Laws of Form.* London: George Allen & Unwin.
Sperry, R. W.
1969. "A Modified Concept of Consciousness." *Psychological Review* 76: 532–36.
1970. "An Objective Approach to Subjective Experience: Further Explanation of a Hypothesis." *Psychological Review* 77: 585–90.
Targ, Russell, and Puthoff, Harold E.
1977. *Mind-Reach: Scientists Look at Psychic Ability.* New York: Delacorte Books.
Tarski, Alfred
1956. *Logic, Semantics, Metamathematics.* Translated by J. H. Woodger. Oxford: Clarendon Press.
Ten Houten, W. D., and Kaplan, C. D.
1973. *Science and Its Mirror Image: A Theory of Inquiry.* New York: Harper & Row.
Thom, René
1975. *Structural Stability and Morphogenesis.* Translated by D. H. Fowler. Reading, Mass.: W. A. Benjamin.
Toulmin, Stephen
1953. *The Philosophy of Science.* New York: Hutchinson.
1974. "The Structure of Scientific Theories." In *The Structure of Scientific Theories,* ed. F. Suppes, pp. 600–14. Urbana: University of Illinois Press.
Trigg, Roger
1973. *Reason and Commitment.* London: Cambridge University Press.
Turbayne, Colin Murray
1962. *The Myth of Metaphor.* New Haven: Yale University Press.
Vygotsky, Lev Semenovich
1962. *Thought and Language.* Translated by E. Hanfmann and C. Vakar. Cambridge: The M. I. T. Press.
Waisman, F.
1962. "The Resources of Language." In *The Importance of Language,* ed. M. Black, pp. 107–20. Ithaca: Cornell University Press.
Warren, Richard M.
1976. "Auditory Illusions and Perceptual Processes." In *Contemporary Issues in Experimental Phonetics,* ed. H. J. Lass, pp. 389–417. New York: Academic Press.
Watzlawick, Paul
1977. *How Real Is Real?* New York: Vintage Books.
Watzlawick, Paul; Beavin, J. H.; and Jackson, D. D.
1967. *Pragmatics of Human Communication.* New York: W. W. Norton.
Watzlawick, Paul; Weakland, John; and Fisch, Richard
1974. *Change: Principles of Problem Formation and Problem Resolution.* New York: W. W. Norton.
Wechsler, Judith, ed.
1978. *On Aesthetics in Science.* Cambridge: The M. I. T. Press.

White, John, ed.
1974. *Frontiers of Consciousness.* New York: Julian Press.
Whitehead, Alfred North
1948. *Science and the Modern World.* New York: The New American Library of World Literature.
Whitehead, Alfred North, and Russell, Bertrand
1927. *Principia Mathematica.* 2nd ed. Cambridge: Cambridge University Press.
Whorf, Benjamin Lee
1956. *Language, Thought and Reality.* Edited by J. B. Carroll. Cambridge: The M. I. T. Press.
Wiener, Norbert
1948. *Cybernetics.* Cambridge: The M. I. T. Press.
Wigner, Eugene
1969. "The Unreasonable Effectiveness of Mathematics in the Natural Sciences." In *The Spirit and the Uses of the Mathematical Sciences.* Edited by T. L. Saaty and F. J. Weyl, pp. 123–40. New York: McGraw-Hill.
1970. *Symmetries and Reflections, Scientific Essays.* Cambridge: The M. I. T. Press.
Wilden, Anthony
1972. *System and Structure.* London: Tavistock.
Wittengenstein, Ludwig
1953. *Philosophical Investigations.* Translated by G. E. M. Anscombe. New York: The Macmillan Co.
1961. *Tractatus Logico-Philosophicus.* Translated by D. F. Pears and B. F. McGuinness. London: Routledge & Kegan Paul.
1966. *Lectures and Conversations on Aesthetics. Psychology and Religious Belief.* Edited by C. Barrett. Berkeley: The University of California Press.
1969. *On Certainty.* Translated by D. Paul and G. E. M. Anscombe. New York: Harper & Row.
1970. *Zettel.* Berkeley: The University of California Press.
Wood, Forrest G.
1954. "Porpoise Play." *Mariner,* March, p. 4. Quoted in Anthony Alpers, *Dolphins,* p. 100. London: John Murray, 1960.
Woodcock, Alexander, and Davis, Monte
1978. *Catastrophe Theory.* New York: E. P. Dutton.
Young, Arthur, and Musès, Charles, eds.
1972. *Consciousness and Reality.* New York: Outerbridge Lazard.
Zeeman, E. C.
1976. "Catastrophe Theory." *Scientific American,* April, 65–83.

INDEX

Abstraction: power of in all organisms, 1–3, 35; selectiveness of, 15–19; exemplified in science by quarks, 25; as classificatory and comparative modes, 98; in degrees of writing, 108–109; with respect to texts, 112–13; why the primacy of, 146–48

Analog-digital distinction, 8, 9–10, 57; defined, 153n; in animal communication, 9–10, 33–35, 116; in perspectival modes, 22; a thought experiment to illustrate, 37–38; with respect to metaphor and metonymy, 52, 61; related to analysis, 71–72; in writing, 108, 109; as modes of communication, 116–17; characteristic of thermostat, 119; in icons as opposed to word strings, 154n; related to Möbius strip, 156n; and nature of genetic code, 162n; related to boundaried spaces and Peircean signs, 163n

. Arbitrariness, 107–109; with respect to human language, 36–37; in games, 37; and transparency, 70; of spider web, 107–108; of writing, 108–109; of graphemes, 113; of sign systems in human culture, 136

Axioms: I, 6; II, 7; III, 8; IV; 8

Boundaried spaces: at the most fundamental level, 6–13; as mental constructs, 14–16; in the act of creativity, 18–19; how the same and how different, 19–21; becoming *differences*, 25–26; in human games, 37–38; mental representation of, 48–51; interaction of in metaphor and metonymy, 53; relation to names, 67; derived from Spencer-Brown and Peirce, 152n; as counterparts to Peirce's icons, 163n; fusion of to form larger boundaried spaces, 163n

Cartesian world views, 141, 161n

Catastrophe: related to Gestalt switches or digital leaps, 58, 60, 81–82; related to catastrophe theory, 156n

Category mistakes, 118; in metaphor and metonymy construction, 43–46; in play activity, 46–48; awareness of necessary for *deembedment*, 98; in reading, 147

Causalist-mechanistic-energetic world view, 141, 142–43

Change: through oscillatory model, 92; in modes of thinking, 102–103; at metalevel, 174

Classification, 134

Code switching: in animal communication, 33–36, 47; with respect to metaphor and metonymy, 48

Conceptual frameworks. *See* Perceptual modes

Condensation: of boundaried spaces, 73–76; related to tacit knowledge, 76–80; of two spaces into a third space, 110–11; and nonconscious expectations, 112; explicit messages have lesser degree of, 117; necessary for accumulation of knowledge, 135; as contrasted with *embedment*, 91, 160n

Contexts and relations: learning depends upon, 80

Continuity-discontinuity. *See* Discontinuity-continuity

Contraction: of boundaried spaces, 92, 93; in metaphor construction, 52–53, 54

Corollaries: I, 8; II, 19; III, 52; IV, 93

Counterarguments: less prevalent in oral cultures, 134; related to argumentative function, 126–28

Countermessages: rudimentary level of, 123–25; at level of descriptive function, 125–26

Countersignals, 123, 124, 125

Counterspaces: related to countermarks in texts, 105–106

Counterstatements: less prevalent in oral cultures, 134; and counterpropositions, as related to descriptive function, 125–26

Countertexts: less prevalent in oral cultures, 134; potential infinity of, 145; follow from opening systems, 146

Cuts: related to boundaried spaces, 152n

de Broglie, Louis, 56

Deconstruction: related to *deembedment*, 165n

SEMIOTIC FOUNDATIONS

Steps toward an Epistemology of Written Texts

By Floyd Merrell

"Writing" *(écriture)* is a fundamentally different activity from "speaking" *(parole)*, and both differ in important ways from "language" *(langue)*. Floyd Merrell's innovative and challenging work applies semiotic theory to the study of written texts, set against a general theory of signs. By "written texts" the author means "all corpora set down in natural or artificial languages for the purpose of conveying hypotheses, ideas, thoughts, observations, reports, intuitions, feelings, and emotions." The notion of semiotic foundations for written texts entails the construction of a conceptual framework with which to account for the perception and conception of signs, from the simplest organisms to human levels.

Firmly grounded in a Peircian approach, the book offers "thought experiments" to recreate in the reader an experience analogous to the creative process itself. Merrell demonstrates that the act of writing bears on universal human capacities for inferential reasoning, for developing learning strategies, and for organizing sense data. In this light, it becomes apparent that writing, while sharing characteristics with other sign forms, is what makes human semiotics most distinctively human.

Semiotic Foundations draws from the philosophy of science, linguistics, literary theory, and other disciplines to present a consistently rigorous exploration of what semiotic analysis can bring to the study of knowledge.